PERSONAL
LEADERSHIP

D1414285

Making a World of Difference
PERSONAL LEADERSHIP
A Methodology of Two Principles and Six Practices

Barbara F. Schaetti, Ph.D.

Sheila J. Ramsey, Ph.D.

Gordon C. Watanabe, Ed.D.

FlyingKite Publications

Seattle, WA

Personal Leadership

FlyingKite Publications is an imprint of Personal Leadership Seminars LLC. For rights and permission, contact: <www.plseminars.com>.

"FlyingKite Publications," "Personal Leadership: Making a World of Difference," and the "Critical Moment Dialogue," are service marks owned by Personal Leadership Seminars LLC. Where abbreviations for these phrases are used (for example, "FlyingKite," "Personal Leadership," "Personal Leadership Seminars," "PL Seminars," "PL," and "CMD"), it is understood that they are used in the context of these service marks.

Editing by Marnie Schaetti, Raido Dynamics
Proofreading by Linda Rasmussen, Proof Positive Communications
Design and artwork by Barbara Burfoot, Verge Design
Cover photographs by Jan O'Brien
All haiku by Heather Robinson

The authors and editor have done their utmost to correctly reference cited materials in both the text and the bibliographic list of recommended reading. Readers noting mistakes are asked to inform the publisher, so that corrections may be made for the next edition.

ISBN 978-0-9797167-0-6

*This book is dedicated to those
who live and work across culture and difference.*

May we, together, realize a positive future for all.

ACKNOWLEDGMENTS

Many people have played a role in bringing Personal Leadership and this book into reality.

We thank our brilliant editor, Marnie Schaetti at Raido Dynamics, whose work on this book was invaluable; our proofreader, Linda Rasmussen at Proof Positive Communications; our designer, Barbara Burfoot at Verge Design Works; and our "book cook," Joanna Parfitt at Summertime Publishing. Their commitment, creativity, and expertise ensure that we send this book out into the world representing our best effort. Thank you all.

We take this opportunity to acknowledge others who actively helped us build and continue to support the organization through which we now do our work, Personal Leadership Seminars LLC. In particular we thank Laura Elfline of Mosaic Solutions, Laurie Rhodes of Copyright Resources, and Donna Stringer of Executive Diversity Services.

We would like to express our deepest gratitude to a teacher, Dawn, with whom we studied. She helped us open to the possibility within us, and to a belief in that possibility. This book then is our gift back to her.

Four organizations served as the birthing grounds for Personal Leadership. We thank them: the Summer Institute for Intercultural Communication (SIIC), Whitworth University, Transition Dynamics, and The Crestone Institute. There are special individuals associated with each to whom we are deeply grateful. At SIIC: Executive Director Janet Bennett, Director Milton Bennett, Associate Director Margaret (Peggy) Pusch, Chris Cartwright, Antimo Cimono, Karen Coleman, John (Jack) Condon, Jef Davis, Sandra Garrison, Bruce La Brack, Mary Mears, Sara Oakland, Rikka Salonen, Dianne Hofner Saphiere, Phyllis Thompson, Franki Trujillo-Dalbey, Greg Walker, Elsa Wallace, Kent Warren, Lori Welch, and Miki Yamashita. At Whitworth: President William Robinson, David Cherry, Dayna Coleman, O.J. Cotes, Gerry Duffy, Auleen Duffy, Peggy Johnsen, Esther Louie, Randy Michaelis, Barb Sanders, Becky Sartell, Dennis

Sterner, and Ginny Whitehouse. At Transition Dynamics and The Crestone Institute: the numerous coaching and team-building clients who contributed their learning over the years. Thank you all for your early and ongoing belief in Personal Leadership.

We also thank our many students whose questions, insights, and commitments to practice have been integral to the evolution of Personal Leadership. In particular our thanks go to our interns at SIIC; our students in the Master in Teaching (MIT) program at Whitworth University; and our students in MAIR (the Master of Arts in Intercultural Relations, a joint degree program of the Intercultural Communication Institute and University of the Pacific). Without you, Personal Leadership would not offer what it does today.

To participants in our Personal Leadership seminars, we say "Wow!" Many of you took an extraordinary leap of faith and traveled to a remote (albeit quite remarkable) place in the southwest corner of Colorado to explore the possibilities. Special appreciation belongs to our first facilitators, five intrepid souls who committed to Personal Leadership before it was a known and tested framework—you are true explorers. Our thanks to you: Esther Louie, Jan O'Brien, Heather Robinson, Megumi Sugihara, and Rita Wuebbeler. We also thank, among the many others too numerous to mention: Jin Abe, Thorunn Bjarnadottir, Lorna Dwyer, Alfred Flores, Vanessa Harris, Tina Johnson, Christoph Jakob, Adair Linn-Nagata, Akiko Moriyama, Shreemathi Ramnath, Elizabeth Robinson, Valerie Scane, Véronique Schoeffel, Monique-Paule Tubb, Kikue Yamamoto, and Alex Yu.

We offer love and appreciation to our parents for giving us each the life circumstances that first inspired this journey: Henry and Rachel Schaetti, D.A. and Sammye Ramsey, and Hideo and Ikuko Dorothy Watanabe. And to our families and special friends, who inspire and support us as we continue onwards: Francine Bélanger, Michael Dobbs, Matthew Eliot, Faye Field, Anne Jorgensen, Mary Val McCoy, Kathryn Poling, Denis Poirier, Susan Schaetti Quail, Michael Ramsey, Erinellene Sanborn, Marnie Schaetti, David Sproul, and all our people around the world and in Ballard, Bern, Crestone, DC, and Spokane.

Finally, our deepest thanksgiving to......42.

Love, joy, and peace.

CONTENTS

LIST OF STORIES

Seeds burst forth, spreading
Across the land. Can there be
Too many flowers?

FOREWORD

Perhaps you, like many of us, have recently experienced a powerful transition. You may have chosen to enter a new culture, and to encounter the delicious richness of often confusing daily surprises. Or, you may have been dragged, kicking and screaming, into unemployment, a medical crisis, or some other personal loss. You may find yourself assigned to an intercultural team, challenged by the seemingly endless complications of negotiating daily tasks. In short, you have chosen to change, or had change thrust upon you.

You may view that change as being positive or negative. It may have erupted into your otherwise tranquil life, or crept in gradually. In any case, you are now faced with the inevitable—and daunting—requirements of a transition, a psychological adaptation to the change that has occurred.

As we navigate such transitions, we summon all the skills, insights, and support systems we can gather. This book has been designed to illuminate that process, and create with you the safety that makes transition an adventure, not a nightmare.

The authors realize that the teachable moments during such demanding contexts often slip past us, lost in the maelstrom of excess stress and a yearning for stability. In effect, what was once out-of-awareness has commanded your attention and you are now acutely conscious that you haven't a clue about what is really going on. Something's up.

A trigger event, where you have reached the edge of your understanding, has occurred. It may be an intercultural event, where your values are assaulted by a stranger ("That's sexist!"). It could be a conflict among diverse team members based on seemingly irrational overreactions ("Why do the virtual meetings have to be on their schedule when it's midnight here?"). It could be your *own* irrational reactions ("I don't care if it's cultural, I hate it!"). Or it may simply be some pleasant but unexpected happening ("Where did *that* come from?").

What matters most is what you choose to do next.

You may choose to escape, in order to avoid sorting out what seems overwhelmingly complex. You may react with frustration, or perhaps prejudice. You might even relax into naiveté, the blissful state that suggests, eventually, this will all go away.

Or you may be curious.

Curiosity can be viewed as a sense of wonder, a "state of mind that signals we have reached the limits of our present understanding and that things may be different from how they look," as described by Paul Martin Opdal.

For interculturalists, knowing that things may be different from how they seem is an everyday occurrence, a source of profound cultural humility. If you truly realize that you may not have the answer, and further, that your truth is merely one way of viewing the world, cultural differences can become a powerful resource.

To call forth culture as a resource requires cultivation of curiosity, the keystone for intercultural competence. When we are inquisitive, the trigger event inspires efforts at sense-making and skill-building. We ask ourselves what is happening within, and we ask others to help us navigate the terrain. We use cultural maps to analyze what we need to know; we use empathy to sense our feelings, and those of others. We seek to develop the necessary skills to bridge the differences. In short, we consciously set about developing cultural self-knowledge and intercultural competence.

For the authors of this book, the inspiration for integrating these principles occurred many years ago, when they began working with particularly challenging groups. They were convinced that synthesizing what we know about the human response to transitions, the power of curiosity, and the potential for intercultural competence would foster high-functioning teams.

At that time, they set about the task of developing intercultural teams, teams that could function under stressful demands, with little sleep, few comforts, and yet maintain highly stimulating and satisfying interactions. They needed teams that could form, storm, norm, and perform across cultures in two weeks, and love it.

The model of Personal Leadership (PL) in this book is the result. Refined over the last decade, Personal Leadership has been implemented in graduate schools, global corporate teams, social justice efforts, study abroad programs, international development teams, summer institutes, and humanitarian relief organizations throughout the world. It is practiced by groups in a wide variety of cultures, who appreciate the conceptual foundation on which the model is based as well as the accessibility of the principles.

Most importantly, the practice of Personal Leadership supports each of us while we face the challenges of the work we do, challenges within ourselves, as well as challenges from others. It diminishes the stress while calling forth the resilience necessary to be curious rather than confounded by inexplicable cultural events.

While the text is subtitled "Making a World of Difference," it might just as easily refer to "What You Make of a World of Difference." Personal Leadership provides a map for navigating that world.

Janet Marie Bennett
Executive Director, Intercultural Communication Institute
Portland, Oregon, USA
July 2007

INTRODUCTION

Dreaming together
We are weaving the unseen
Into becoming.

Does it ever strike you as amazing that here we are, in the 21st century, still picking fights with one another, still going to war? Certainly some of our disagreements are about issues of vital consequence such as economic opportunity, social justice, the preservation and distribution of natural resources, and personal and religious freedom. However, whether with neighbors close by on the other side of the street or far away on the other side of the world, we often seem to turn to violence—military, economic, environmental—as an option of first resort. Doesn't this seem to you just a little bit ludicrous, maybe even incredibly wasteful? Something so much more interesting is possible!

This book is about what's possible. From our hearts to yours, it introduces Personal Leadership as a pathway towards a peaceable world.

"Please!" you may be saying. "What a grandiose vision!" And indeed, it is. Yet a dynamically peaceable world is the song being sung by hearts all over this planet.

We think it's time to get over the idea that we can just keep arguing and going to war when our differences get the better of us. It's time to use our differences as a creative resource.

When people come together from different backgrounds or with different perspectives and opinions, an inherently creative possibility exists. One of the most profound things we can do as humans today is open to that creative possibility. We can learn to respond to people whose ways are foreign to us not by turning away, but by drawing closer, both to them and to ourselves. We can learn to transform differences from walls that separate into bridges that connect. Instead of shutting down in fear or mistrust, we can learn to choose growth and new possibility.

As the old adage says, "Peace begins with me." The same is true here: responding to difference as a creative resource begins with each of us.

Daring to Hold a Vision

This book is about daring to hold a vision of a peaceable world. It's about daring to hold a vision in which we use differences to build bridges between us, and it's about daring to bring that vision home into our lives, right here, right now. It's about using Personal Leadership to help us translate the *idea* of peace into the *practice* of peace.

Imagine living in world where…

You and I and people everywhere choose to learn from situations we find uncomfortable. Perhaps the person with whom we're interacting is in some way different from us, or we're in the midst of major personal or professional transition. Whatever the reason, we use our discomfort with the new and unfamiliar as an alarm clock, as a call to pay attention. Instead of shutting down, we deliberately open up to learning something new, even perhaps to changing something fundamental about how we think or feel.

You and I and people everywhere skillfully negotiate our differences so that we promote mutual respect and well-being. We notice when we disagree, when tensions start to rise, when we have different assumptions and ways of doing things. Instead of assigning blame, we take a breath and look for the truth that connects us.

You and I and people everywhere discern our right action when confronted by myriad choices. We don't just do what we've always done or do what others are doing, just because. When we feel uncertain or even confused, we turn to our deep inner wisdom. We intentionally ask for guidance, knowing and trusting that, having asked, we will understand our next best step.

And imagine living in a world where…

You and I and people everywhere cultivate an expanded sense of what is possible and what deeply matters to us. We commit to living our lives as creators of our own reality. We commit to separating external circumstances from our internal experience of them. When we notice ourselves feeling like victims—victims of a rainy day, victims of a tough economy—we look for the opportunity that's being offered to bring forth positive change for ourselves and for others, and step into our creator energy.

You and I and people everywhere sustain the kind of mutual inquiry that's necessary to address complex global concerns. We talk together not to defend our positions or to persuade the other to agree. We talk together to get clarification and to explore possibilities, to build new meaning together.

You and I and people everywhere reach across animosity and misunderstanding toward connection and common purpose. We recognize that just as our differences can serve as separating walls, so too can they serve as connecting bridges. Instead of turning away, we step out onto the bridge and walk together.

We dare to hold this vision of a peaceable world. What vision are you daring to hold? Is it as grandiose as ours? We hope so! Does it make your heart sing? Ours does!

Is it possible to bring forth a vision like this? Without a doubt. This book offers the methodology of Personal Leadership to help each of us on our journeys to do so. It outlines Personal Leadership's two principles, six practices and the powerful process technology called the Critical Moment Dialogue (CMD).

Personal Leadership Integrative Stories

We have chosen two stories to present to you here. As with all the stories in the book, they were submitted to us by real people writing about their real experiences. While we've occasionally edited for clarity, the only substantive changes we've made have been, sometimes, to the names of the people involved.

As you read each story, starting now with the two that follow, can you identify what the protagonist is doing? What do you begin to understand about Personal Leadership?

INTERNATIONAL STUDENT ORIENTATION

by Jin

I am responsible for international student orientations on my university campus. An international student from the Netherlands told a friend of hers, "I don't see why I had to attend the orientation. It was a waste of time." The friend then came to my office and shared the story with me.

As I listened, my body tensed up ever so slightly. Then I felt defensive. My immediate judgment was, "Well, that's why many students get into trouble with immigration and academic policies later on." The next minute, I thought, "Hold that judgment!"

I excused myself, saying I'd be right back, and went into the hallway outside my office where I have a poster on the wall showing a sunrise over the ocean; I keep it there to help me to relax. Once I looked at it, I felt as if I stepped out of the emotional bubble that I was about to be caught in, and suddenly had many thoughts starting to pop up.

After a minute, I went back into my office and told the woman who was speaking to me, "If that is her perspective, I humbly respect that and would like to talk to her about it."

I realized several things. I have been to three schools in the United States as an international student myself and have never attended an orientation. So who am I to criticize other international students for not wanting to participate? When I came to my current university, I wrote a letter to the school asking for an exemption from orientation because I already "knew it all"—and the exemption was granted. Maybe this student is in the same situation. I don't know. What else do I not know about this student?

Allowing myself to experience, even to deliberately invite, the ambiguity of the situation shifted everything into a much easier place. Instead of doing something about the Dutch student from a place of tense defensiveness that judged her as wrong, I'll be able to do my job as I would like to do it and explore the possibilities and options with her.

CORPORATE COACHING

by Susan

I was hired to provide performance coaching for a team that is part of a multinational corporation. Steve is the USAmerican leader, most of the members are German, and all of them are based in Germany. As soon as I met Steve, I knew he was a big part of the team's problem: he cut people off in discussions, he whined, he was insulting, he reframed everything negatively.

As I watched him interact with his team, I could feel my dislike of him get stronger and stronger. He was clearly a terrible leader, and pretty quickly I had two pages of notes tracking everything he was doing wrong. I was looking forward to meeting with him privately, to going through my notes in detail until he really understood what an awful impact his negativity was having on the team.

All of a sudden, I noticed the sense of adrenalin in my body and my feelings of righteous anticipation. I took a breath, several breaths. I saw all the judgments I was making about Steve being a terrible leader and an awful person. I decided to make a point of talking with him during the morning break. It turns out he has a son about whom he's very proud—his whole face lit up when he talked about him. I went for a walk with Steve during the lunch break. The physical movement helped me a lot and so did seeing Steve's appreciation of the German countryside.

During the afternoon session, Steve's German team members gave him very direct feedback on his behavior. He sat there impassively; it seemed obvious that he still wasn't understanding that he was the team's main problem. Even so, when we met after dinner for a private coaching session I decided to consider the possibility that I might be wrong. Instead of pulling out my list of his terrible behaviors, I asked him how he was doing with the team's feedback. He said he had had no clue about the impact his behavior was having, that he was devastated. He became animated as he described how he'd had to go back to his hotel room to call his wife, to talk to his son, to remember that he was loved. He asked me what he could do to be a better leader, and we proceeded to have a very positive coaching session.

I'm glad I remembered why I do this work, that it's about bringing forth the best of what my clients have to offer, and that I didn't just plow forward with my list of Steve's wrongs.

What are the common themes in these stories? What were the protagonists doing? How were they able to transform differences of perspective and belief from walls that separate into bridges that connect? How did they notice when they wanted to shut down in anger or mistrust? How did they instead choose to open to new learning and possibility?

Using the language of Personal Leadership that we introduce in this book, Jin and Susan were:

1. attending to judgment
2. attending to emotion
3. attending to physical sensation
4. cultivating stillness
5. engaging ambiguity
6. aligning with vision

Both of these protagonists deliberately chose growth and new possibility in the face of the unfamiliar. Both of them chose to promote mutual respect and well-being. They caught themselves in an automatic tendency to assign blame and instead chose mutual inquiry, a connection to common purpose, and the guidance of deep wisdom. Personal Leadership helped them hold the vision. It helped them translate the idea of peace into the practice of peace, and, through that process, to discern their own right action for the situation in which they found themselves.

As we have said, that's what this book is about.

Acknowledging Our Roots

The vision we hold, and the pathway towards it called Personal Leadership, has deep and broad roots. It is inspired by two seemingly disparate sources of wisdom. We draw on a range of age-old philosophic, religious, and esoteric traditions, including mystic forms of Christianity, Buddhism, Hinduism, Judaism, and Islam. We also draw on contemporary interdisciplinary studies such as intercultural communication, leadership development, whole-person self-development, education, positive psychology, and the quantum sciences.

Together these traditions emphasize three key points:

1. To be effective in our interactions with others, not least in negotiating differences between us, we have first to know ourselves.
2. To have guidance in times of uncertainty and in environments of continuous change, we must intentionally cultivate the "leader within."
3. To live a creative life, we must commit to practices that still the mind and that support self-reflection, self-management, and self-motivation.

Our work with Personal Leadership brings together these perspectives in our belief that a choice is present in all moments, a choice for self-reflection, self-development, and creative collaboration. We further believe that this choice is especially present in those moments made vibrant by the differences in values, worldviews, and behaviors of those involved. When we choose self-reflection, self-development, and creative collaboration, we unlock transformative possibilities for everyone.

We three authors count ourselves blessed for having had the opportunity to experience the power and possibility inherent in Personal Leadership. We have personally lived our way into the methodology. Barbara, a dual-national with one Swiss parent and one European-American parent, grew up in 10 countries on five continents by the age of 18 and moved internationally 12 times by the age of 22; both her parents were born in India and lived internationally mobile childhoods themselves. Sheila, European-American and raised in the United States, moved frequently as a child from one culturally distinct region of the country to another; she has spent 25 years of her professional life relating to Japan. Gordon is sansei, a third-generation Japanese-American, raised in a predominantly European-American world wherein he and his brother were the only children of Asian ancestry in their school; his parents met while they were in a Japanese internment camp in the United States during World War II. All three of us have careers that focus on domestic diversity and/or international relations, efforts that take us all over the world.

The framework presented in this book, made public in its first iteration in 1998, actually emerged in 1995 as we began to ask ourselves some rather pointed questions: Why do those who sincerely care about interacting effectively with people different from themselves nevertheless have such a hard time doing so? What ways of being and doing might give specific, strategic direction for turning the theory of interacting across difference into practice? How can and do people hold themselves open to the fullness of their creative capacity, even when they are confronted by uncertainty, confusion, and cultural chaos?

From the very beginning, we were joined in a committed investigation of answers to these questions by innumerable clients, students, and colleagues. Through them, and through our own lived exploration, evolved what we are now presenting to you as Personal Leadership. We have had a joyful journey, and we anticipate a long and fruitful path still ahead.

Making a World of Difference

You may have noticed this part of the book's title: "Making a World of Difference." It holds two meanings for us, and we offer both of them to you as complementary aspects of the book's core message.

One meaning of the phrase focuses on how we choose to look at the differences that exist between us. When we are willing to look at them directly, and to recognize that they don't necessarily make us good or bad but simply different, then the ways in which we differ become interesting, exciting, even valuable. We become less reliant on emphasizing similarities and more eager to discover the creative resource that our differences provide. A whole new world begins to open up. Complexity becomes our ally. We start to make a fascinating world for ourselves, through the lens of difference.

The complimentary meaning of the phrase asserts that we can make a positive difference in the world, and in our local and global communities. As we disentangle from our assumptions and expectations and invite deep discernment into our daily experience, we increase our skill as change agents. We become able to act for social justice and environmental well-being, bringing forth the positive change we envision for ourselves and for the world.

As you go forward and read this book, we wish you the full possibility and great joy that comes with "making a world of difference."

Barbara, Sheila, and Gordon
July 2007

A Note on Sources

We reference throughout the book the writings of various scholars and practitioners whose work relates to Personal Leadership. Rather than using footnotes, we have decided to include their names and their pertinent publication(s) in the flow of text. All sources, as well as other material of potential interest, can be found in the Recommended Reading section at the end of the book. Similarly, URLs for the websites of organizations we reference are included in our Websites of Interest section.

Part One

INTRODUCING

PERSONAL LEADERSHIP

In this section, we introduce the basic ideas that drive Personal Leadership.

In Chapter 1, we describe Personal Leadership as a methodology of two principles and six practices. We discuss its purpose, and how it can serve us in a complex, globalized world where differences, change, and the unfamiliar are increasingly part of our daily experience. We explain the relationship between Personal Leadership and six core themes:

1. leading from the inside out
2. using difference as a creative resource
3. emphasizing self-reflection
4. choosing our internal state of being
5. beginning with ourselves
6. committing to applied competence

We use a lot of stories in this book to illustrate what we're talking about. As with the Personal Leadership integrative stories we presented in the Introduction, they all describe real events experienced by real people. Sometimes the stories were written by the Personal Leadership practitioner directly involved, sometimes the stories were told to us and we wrote them down. Where requested to protect the privacy of others in the stories (friends, clients), we've changed the practitioner's name and other identifying characteristics. About half of the stories are from our own lives, the lives of the book's three authors.

It's important to know that the stories included in the book are offered to you because we, the 22 practitioners who contributed them, value what we learned. Through using Personal Leadership, experiences that otherwise might be embarrassing, or so normal as to be boring, become powerful learning moments. When that happens, initial hesitation about sharing them tends to disappear. That which was boring or embarrassing becomes instead deeply meaningful and a reason for celebration.

In Chapter 2, we introduce you to the two principles of Personal Leadership, mindfulness and creativity. It's in this chapter that we start offering you "Try This" activities. All of these activities are designed to help you deepen your understanding of what you're reading.

CHAPTER ONE

What is Personal Leadership?

I give up, am still.
The elusive cat settles
In my open lap.

Personal Leadership (PL) offers two principles and six practices. Its purpose is to help us stay connected to inspiration even when we're faced with the new and unfamiliar.

Instead of reacting to people whose ways are foreign to us by turning away, Personal Leadership helps us draw closer to them and to ourselves. Personal Leadership helps us bring forth our highest levels of learning and creativity. Instead of shutting down in fear or mistrust, it helps us open to the possibilities that exist when we find ourselves in situations that do not fit our expectations, experiences, hopes, or desires. Instead of naively insisting that people act more like us, do it more our way, Personal Leadership sustains us by helping us choose growth, personal development, and real professional competence.

We call this "Personal Leadership" because it's about taking leadership of our personal experience.

Leading From the Inside Out

What does the word "leadership" mean to you?

To many, it implies a focus on those who are leaders in the conventional sense: the head of a team, the parent of the family, the teacher in the classroom, the conductor of the orchestra. Increasingly, however, those contributing to the contemporary literature on extraordinary leadership such as Joseph Jaworsky, Peter Senge, and Margaret Wheatley, have broadened the definition. These scholars and practitioners define leadership as a core competence for everyone, whether or not we're ever in the formal position of leading others.

Leadership is, at root, about understanding and managing our own internal experience. Extraordinary leaders know that experience is subjective: we feel and think and behave in the way we do, we see what we see and hear what we hear, because of the way we've been taught by our families, our schools, our cultures. In *Managing Diversity,* Lee Gardenswartz and Anita Rowe say that we each have our own particular subjective "cultural programming" that drives us to certain assumptions and expectations. We develop automatic reactions that influence us to feel and think and behave in our habitual ways however new or unfamiliar the circumstances may be.

The practices of Personal Leadership help us notice all of this. They help us notice our automatic reactions and untangle from them. The practices help us learn from our ingrained habits so that, even though we may still have our automatic reactions, instead of them leading us, we are in charge of them. That means that we can more mindfully and creatively respond to the particular situation we're in, to the other person or event. The more mindful and creative we are, especially when we're in an unfamiliar environment, the more chance we have of being effective. All it takes is the commitment to be the leader of our own lives and a willingness to engage in the moment-to-moment practice.

Being responsible for ourselves in this way is where formal leadership begins; it's the first step in being able to effectively lead others. It's also the first step in being able to respond to difference as a creative resource and to the unfamiliar as an opportunity.

Leadership is, at root, about understanding and managing our own internal experience.

Using Difference as a Creative Resource

One very common response to people whose opinions and behaviors are different from ours is to want them to be more like us. As Milton Bennett writes in *Basic Concepts of Intercultural Communication,* it's a natural response. If the people we're dealing with won't or can't or don't become more like us, we tend to judge them as wrong and ourselves as right. The more these people are strangers to us, the more wrong we tend to make them and the more right we tend to make ourselves.

On the most basic level, what we mean by "people different from ourselves" is people who don't see things the same way we do, who don't act the same way we would act if we were in similar circumstances.

Sometimes we go into a new situation with someone and we're already assuming that he's different from us. Maybe he has a different color skin, or a different language or accent, or a different passport, or even just a different way of dressing. Sometimes we discover that someone is different from us only after we've been talking or working together for a while. We realize that something she's doing (or not) is really driving us nuts, or even that something we are doing (or not) is offensive to her. Maybe it's not even that clear. Maybe we just notice that we're confused, that there seems to be an undercurrent of meaning that we're not picking up on. We find ourselves thinking that the other person isn't doing what we believe a normal person should do, or say, or think, or feel—he's irrational, we say; she's strange.

The online MSN Encarta dictionary says difference is "the state of being unlike others: the quality of being different from or unlike something or somebody else." In the modern world, we tend to think about difference in terms of categories like nationality, language and language fluency, race and ethnicity, gender, physical ability, age or generation, sexual orientation, religious tradition and spiritual practice, profession or occupation, political affiliation, education, socioeconomic status, recreational preferences and hobbies.... The list could, and indeed does, go on and on. Situations of difference come up with the person sitting next to us on the subway; they take place in the middle of a family reunion; they occur in neighborhoods and communities within our own country; and they are easy to find across international negotiation tables. When we talk about difference, we're talking about all of this. In particular, we are talking about the deep levels of difference where values, beliefs, and behaviors come into play.

Situations of difference don't always involve other people. They also exist whenever we find ourselves facing the new and unfamiliar. They are presented to us when we leave a job, take on a new project or start a new school, get married or divorced, or move to a different country.

This is a good time to emphasize what some of you may already be thinking: not all of us respond to differences by shutting down. Some of us, of course, find differences enormously stimulating and energizing. Our hearts expand when we hear a different language spoken, see someone visually distinct from ourselves, or find ourselves suddenly participating in some unexpected greeting ritual.

It is because so many of us find differences enormously exciting that we travel abroad on holiday, host international students in our homes, take an overseas posting or a job in an unknown part of our own country, marry our polar opposite, have friends of different ethnicities and religious practices, look for challenging projects to take on at work. We who do this tend to feel tremendously alive when confronted with difference, all our antennae at maximum attention as we revel in the new. Hal Gregerson, who has written extensively about how to maximize success among global executives, recalled this quality of expatriate aliveness when he spoke at the Women on the Move Conference in London, England, in March 2000. There's nothing like being a stranger in a strange land to eliminate the risk of boredom!

Even when this describes us, however, we still have times when we hit a brick wall, those times when being in the midst of difference is no longer stimulating but just frustrating, no longer exciting but simply offensive. Whatever the circumstances, navigating difference has suddenly become a bit more troublesome.

In reality, most of us probably move back and forth along the continuum of response to difference. At times, we respond by staying open and making choices, and at others, we respond by shutting down and turning away. We tend to find differences stimulating when they help us arrive at a new or better idea; we tend to find them offensive when it seems they are blocking our progress toward some goal.

Shutting down in the face of difference doesn't make us bad people—it just makes us human. Even when we've studied such disciplines as intercultural relations, interpersonal communication, mediation and dispute resolution, negotiation and diplomacy, it's still very difficult to engage difference as a creative resource, to turn the theory of it all into day-to-day practice. However well-intentioned we may be, our default tendency is still, at least when we're under pressure, to shut down in the face of difference. Once shut down, on retreat, it's nearly impossible to access our creative core. If we can't access our creative core, we're left with only our habitual thought processes and behaviors to call upon. And that's the challenge: if we're in situations that are unfamiliar to us, or with people very different from those we're used to, then acting in our usual ways when the moment is, in fact, unusual, won't do us or the situation much good.

We tend to find differences stimulating
when they help us arrive at a new or better idea;
we tend to find them offensive when it seems they are
blocking our progress toward some goal.

Emphasizing Self-Reflection

Leading from the inside out and using difference as a creative resource begins with self-reflection. Practicing Personal Leadership requires us to self-reflect with absolute honesty and integrity. We have to be willing to look at our motivations, our assumptions, our expectations. We have to be willing to recognize when we're feeling self-righteous, and we have to be willing to let go of being so sure that we're right, that ours is the only possible truth.

You'll see some of this illustrated in the following story. Linda wrote this as part of an assignment while she was on a study abroad experience in Central America sponsored by her university. Notice how she uses honest self-reflection in this situation with her host mother. She takes leadership of her own values and beliefs and, through that, she's able to creatively respond to a difficult situation of difference.

MEDICAL ADVICE

by Linda

The rash on my leg had been getting progressively worse, and when my host mom saw it one day, she decided that I needed to put her all-natural *medicina* on it. I tried to explain to her that it was okay—I had a cream that I was using, I was sure it would get better. This made no difference as Dona Berta went off to find the *medicina*. I wasn't sure what to do next. Should I protest further or let it go?

I was annoyed and frustrated that she kept pushing the *medicina* on me. And my body itched almost everywhere, and was tired from the activities of the day. I could tell that I was getting more and more rude each time I tried to refuse her help. That made me pause, because I realized I didn't want to let the situation hurt the relationship I had been building with my host family. I knew from what Dona Berta had said that the *medicina* was not cheap for them, so her offering it wasn't just something casual. I made one last feeble attempt at "Esta bien—it's okay" when she came back, but decided to give it up when both my host brother and host father told me I could trust Dona Berta not to hurt me.

I realized that to refuse the help would be a great offense to all of them. In fact, I realized that this wasn't really about the *medicina* (I wasn't going to swallow anything; it wasn't going to be dangerous to me even if it wasn't any good). My refusal of the *medicina* was actually based on my assumption that I had to be extra careful about anything offered to me locally because it wouldn't be up to the standards of western medicine. I realized what an attitude of superiority this was on my part, a "we know better than you do" response.

And so I thanked Dona Berta and let her smooth the *medicina* all over my legs. Later that day, she said my legs seemed much better and I, too, thought they were maybe a little less red. Over the next few days, the rash began to go away. Later on, Dona Berta showed me some information about the *medicina*. It turns out that when she had been telling me about the main ingredient, she had been saying it was aloe vera. I just hadn't recognized the name in Spanish.

Linda was demonstrating real competence here. She noticed when she was starting to shut down in the face of difference, and paid attention to how her own cultural values and assumptions were driving her automatic reactions. She considered whether those first reactions were appropriate for this situation and what the implications might be if she behaved differently. She took leadership of her experience and, believing something better was possible, chose to change her behavior to respond more creatively to the situation she was in.

Throughout this process, Linda was intensely self-reflective; at no time, however, did she self-disclose. She was absolutely honest with herself about her beliefs and attitudes and how they were influencing her behavior, but she never said anything about any of that to her host family. This is a really important distinction to make: practicing Personal Leadership requires us to be intensely self-reflective, but it never requires us to self-disclose.

> *We have to be willing to recognize when*
> *we're feeling self-righteous,*
> *and we have to be willing to let go of being*
> *so sure that we're right.*

Choosing Our Internal State of Being

One of the basic premises of Personal Leadership is that our energetic state is a matter of choice. Whether we feel energized and expanded, on one end of the continuum, or shut down and contracted, on the other, is ultimately a choice we make. More to the point, it's a choice that has profound consequences as we engage across differences and in situations that are unfamiliar to us.

The relatively new field of positive psychology and, in particular, research by Barbara Fredrickson and her colleagues, documents that emotions such as joy, interest, hope, inspiration, contentment, appreciation, and gratitude help us build new skills and intellectual resources. When we hold ourselves in those emotional states, we become smarter and wiser, and we are more open to new ideas and the exploration of possibilities. These kinds of "positive"—what we prefer to call "expanding"—emotions prompt us to rely less on everyday, automatic behaviors, scripts, or habits. They help us pursue novel and creative paths of thought and action. We become more flexible about establishing categories, and less likely to pigeonhole people or situations into right or wrong, good or bad. We become more able to deal with the complexities of change and difference. Cultivating and maintaining an expanded emotional core leads us to see relationship and connection between thoughts and ideas, and to process information in a more integrated fashion.

You can probably imagine what the research is showing about the benefits of expanded emotions on the immune system and therefore on overall resilience, physical health, and well-being. Glen Rein and his colleagues offer the results of one study in their article, "The Physiological and Psychological Effects of Compassion and Anger," published in the *Journal of Advancement in Medicine*. It documents the power of self-induced expanded emotions to minimize the otherwise immune-suppressing effects of challenging situations. The National Resilience Resource Center website offers a good summary of additional research in this area.

At the other end of the emotional continuum, "negative"—what we call "focusing"—emotions also serve a purpose. Emotions like fear, anger, dread, panic, despair, confusion, and blame let us know we're outside our comfort zone. Their purpose biologically is to help us make decisions and to react quickly when our safety is threatened.

Personal Leadership asks us to understand the different purposes served by these two ends of the emotional continuum and to make conscious choices about the internal state that we hold.

When we find ourselves feeling emotions like fear, panic, and blame, Personal Leadership asks us to pause, turn around, and look at them: why do we feel this way? What is it about the circumstance we're in that has us responding as if we're being threatened? Are we, in fact, being threatened, or are we simply being confronted by the new and unfamiliar, by uncertainty and ambiguity? We may automatically react with focusing emotions even when our situation actually requires from us the kind of response that only comes from an expanded emotional state.

There are longer-term implications in the choices we make; it's not just about the kind of response that we need to call upon now. Making the choice to cultivate and maintain an expanded emotional state today not only feels good in the moment, but increases the likelihood that we will feel good in the future. Why? Because we become able to recover more quickly from the effects of fear, anger, and despair. The more we authentically reconnect with expanded emotions, returning, for example, to a sense of calm after worry, the more readily we are able to do it next time. We strengthen our emotional muscle. Our emotional resilience is increased.

Moreover, the research in positive psychology suggests that emotional resilience, reinforced by an authentically expanded emotional state, promotes physical resilience too. The more we choose to cultivate and maintain an expanded emotional state as we live and work in situations of difference, the more we literally protect our health. As expanded emotions help us recover from the physically damaging effects of anger and fear, we protect our hearts and boost our immune systems.

Fredrickson's review of the research also suggests that expanded emotions strengthen our social resources as well as our emotional and physical ones. We form supportive relationships more readily, including across situations of difference, and recover from the loss of social support systems more quickly.

We may automatically react with focusing emotions
even when our situation actually requires from us
the kind of response that only comes from
an expanded emotional state.

Beginning With Ourselves

As you can tell by now, Personal Leadership puts our attention very specifically on us. We take leadership, engage differences, and reflect by beginning with ourselves.

Personal Leadership recognizes that we live in an interdependent and complex world. It is impossible not to communicate; everything we say and do, and indeed on some level even everything we think, is a form of communication. While practicing Personal Leadership is therefore very relational, its focus begins with the "self" rather than with the "other."

Even when—or perhaps especially when—someone does something that hurts or offends us, Personal Leadership does not focus us on what the other person did or did not do, should or should not do. Rather, no matter how provocative the other person or situation may be, Personal Leadership focuses us on attending to our own automatic reactions. Only then, once we have untangled from that reaction and achieved a new level of openness, does Personal Leadership focus us on saying or doing anything directly in response to the other. And whether we in fact say or do anything depends on what we've discerned in that moment as the right thing for *that* moment.

A BUSINESS REPORT

by Francesca

I received an e-mail one day in which someone directly challenged a strong opinion I had about a particular piece of a report I'd written. I immediately felt very angry, hurt, and offended. I began to think about how I would defend my position.

All at once, I noticed that my chest and shoulders felt constricted, my adrenalin was pumping. This led me to recognize the emotions that had swept me up. I remember this particularly because it wasn't usual for me at the time to observe my anger and defensiveness instead of being lost in them.

As soon as I paid attention to what I was feeling, I began to relax, to feel open and curious.

I realized that the e-mail was actually an exciting opportunity. Here was someone with a different opinion! I saw that neither of us was wrong, that we just had different takes on the same situation. I wondered about her thoughts and wanted to know more. So when I wrote back and then later when we spoke, I was able to ask her questions about her perspective. That set a whole different tone, for me and for her, and we had a very creative discussion.

Ultimately, we came up with a solution so much stronger than either of us originally had in mind.

When we're in a situation like Francesca's, most of us put our attention on the other person, what she did, how she did it. We wonder how she could have possibly been so offensive. Wasn't she taught to be respectful of other people, of their work and effort? How could she be so mean? We look for people to whom we can complain about the other person, people who will sympathize with us and agree with us and help us strategize how to "deal" with her.

Personal Leadership helps us do something quite a bit different. It helps us do what Francesca did: pause for a moment when we start to feel righteous and bring our attention back to ourselves. Why are we angry? What are we assuming? What were we expecting? Once Francesca made the connection between feeling angry at her colleague's comments and feeling superior because her position was the only possible good one, she was able to relax and open up with excitement to the difference of opinion. And from that openness, they created an even better solution together than they could have done individually. That's what we mean by using difference as a creative resource!

Now of course sometimes you need to stand up against what somebody is saying or doing, stand up for a moral or humane principle. What Personal Leadership shows us, once we've been practicing for a while, is that we get a whole lot better at standing up for what we believe when we first free ourselves from our own automatic reactions. When they cloud our perceptions and we haven't yet checked to see what deeper cultural value is influencing us, we're going to be much less able to talk with the other person in a way that the person can understand.

That's why Personal Leadership begins with us. Only then does it look at the other person and the action we may need to take to deal with the situation in a competent way.

Practicing Personal Leadership
begins with the "self" rather than with the "other."

Committing to Applied Competence

Personal Leadership is all about competence. It's about being effective in the world as friends, colleagues, neighbors, employees, leaders—in short, as people. If we all lived alone on a desert island or on top of a mountain, we might not need Personal Leadership. As it is, interpersonal interactions are challenging enough, but when you add cultural differences to the mix, add the fast pace of change, add a life filled with uncertainty and with the new and unfamiliar, Personal Leadership becomes a very useful tool.

A lot of us have had very successful relationships across cultural differences. We've made friends with people from the other side of the planet and have worked well with colleagues who have very different approaches to the job. It's pretty safe to say that we've also all had failures in this regard, people with whom we just couldn't connect, from whom we pulled away, whom we offended (although maybe we didn't always know why), or who offended us. Why are we successful in some instances and not in others? Often it's just a matter of luck. We were lucky that in those particular instances our knowledge of working with other cultures, our experience resolving differences, or our mutual commitment to whatever we were doing together outweighed the tension of our differences.

With Personal Leadership, it's no longer a matter of luck: it's a matter of application and practice. Personal Leadership recognizes that understanding what to do when faced with the unfamiliar (knowledge) and actually doing it (competence) are two very different things. This is especially true when our deeply held values or sense of identity are being pushed by cultural difference. Personal Leadership offers a set of practices and a process technology called the Critical Moment Dialogue specifically oriented to bridging this gap between knowledge and competence.

In her story, below, Thorunn talks about how her intercultural competence has grown since she started practicing Personal Leadership.

COMMUNICATING AT WORK

by Thorunn

Using Personal Leadership has helped me become a very practical and creative solution-building person when I deal with people whose ways are unfamiliar and downright strange to me.

I'm able to stay in the moment. I'm able to ask practical questions that shed light on the underlying assumptions that are at play, both mine and theirs. I'm also more able to stay open to possibilities that do not present themselves when viewing a situation from only one angle. I am much more comfortable with not knowing, and I trust that new knowledge of what is possible in every situation will come through my work with a person from a different culture.

I am becoming a better practitioner of authentic listening and dialogue, instead of exchanging opinions, which was the way I used to hold conversations. I have had some exciting moments, when I experienced a new and deep understanding of a situation because of our genuine dialogue, and it was very satisfying to me and the person I was working with. Both our horizons of possibility were expanded.

To me, this is a process, and my experience of it is that it's ongoing. The process is definitely about reaching inside myself and connecting with whatever it is—inner fortitude, gold, or, as I have come to think of it, a "sparkly vibrating thing." I don't think there will be a day when I can say "Now I have understood it all," nor do I wish that day to come.

So I guess I'm saying that the work we do with people whose ways are different and unfamiliar to us is an exciting crossroads of new knowledge brought forth in raw and creative ways. Both people will walk away with a richer and deeper understanding of themselves, and they will have a brand new solution to a project that neither of them thought possible while working alone.

As we have said, being competent across cultures and in unfamiliar situations does not seem to be a natural quality of the human psyche. You only have to look back through history to see how humanity responds to difference. Even those of us with experience across cultures and with deep commitment to the well-being of all have to take a leadership orientation. We have to be willing to choose competence rather than just to hope for it or trust it to luck. Personal Leadership believes that this choice is present in every moment. When we make the choice, magnificent possibilities arise for everyone.

> *Personal Leadership recognizes that*
> *understanding what to do when faced with the*
> *unfamiliar (knowledge) and actually doing it*
> *(competence) are two very different things.*

To Summarize

Personal Leadership is a methodology of two principles and six practices designed to help us stay connected to inspiration even when we are faced with the new and unfamiliar.

Practicing Personal Leadership means:
- taking leadership of our own experience, from the inside out
- engaging difference as a creative resource
- becoming skilled at learning through self-reflection
- authentically choosing the energetic state that will strengthen our creative response
- beginning with a focus on ourselves
- committing to developing our personal and professional competence

CHAPTER TWO

The Two Principles

Was lost in the woods
Love and truth whisper the way
Heart overflowing.

Two principles form the foundation of the Personal Leadership methodology. *Mindfulness* is about being aware, being "awake," and paying attention. *Creativity* is about bringing forth what's right for the particular moment and cultivating our connection to our deepest source of joy and inspiration.

Principles of Personal Leadership

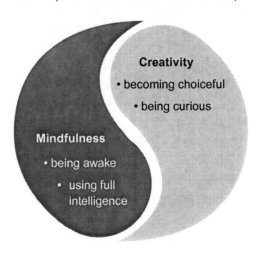

Creativity
• becoming choiceful
• being curious

Mindfulness
• being awake
• using full intelligence

As you'll discover in this chapter, the two principles are interdependent and mutually connected. Each informs the other, each sustains the other, each helps to call forth the other.

Where the two principles of Personal Leadership come together, we find presence, the tangible experience of embodied aliveness. Visualize the Ouroboros, the dragon of mythic symbology that, in eating its tail, is said to represent the link between all things. Likewise, mindfulness and creativity together nurture our capacity for presence, while our capacity for presence emerges out of our expression of mindfulness and creativity.

Mindfulness

A lot has been written about mindfulness over the years. It describes a way of being in the world that most of the great spiritual and philosophic traditions have encouraged for centuries. In the last 15 years, mindfulness has begun making its mark as a secular practice through the writings, for example, of Daniel Goleman in the field of leadership, of Jon Kabat-Zinn in health care, of Ellen Langer in education, and of Stella Ting-Toomey in intercultural communication.

Mindfulness: A Quality of Presence

Leadership guru Daniel Goleman has a wonderful way to define mindfulness. During a presentation he gave at Washington National Cathedral in November 2005, he spoke about it as a "precise non-reactive awareness." The purpose, he says, is to free ourselves from powerful self-defeating emotional habits.

M.C. Richards, in her book *Centering in Pottery, Poetry and the Person,* uses "consciousness" instead of mindfulness. She says:

It takes a heap of resolve to keep from going to sleep in the middle of the show. It's not that we want to sleep our lives away. It's that it requires certain kinds of energy...certain real powers of body and soul to be a match for reality. That's why knowledge and consciousness are two quite different things. Knowledge is like a product we consume or store. All we need are good closets. By consciousness I mean a state of being "awake" to the world throughout our organism. This...requires not closets but an organism attuned to the finest perceptions and responses (p. 15).

When we're living and working with people different from ourselves, when we're faced with situations that are new and unfamiliar and perhaps even a little frightening, "being awake to the world throughout our organism" can support us even when we don't have the necessary knowledge for the situation we're facing. That was true for Sheila in the following story.

BARGAINING AT THE MARKET

by Sheila

I have lived and worked most of my life in the industrialized world, primarily in the United States and Japan, and have been socialized to a certain way of shopping and determining the price of goods. I remember when I first spent time in a city where I had to bargain for the majority of the purchases I made at the local market. At first it was fun. Then it became annoying. The interactions became choked, unpleasantly filled with my instantaneous judgment about whether or not I was being cheated by the vendor who seemed so gleeful in his enjoyment of my ignorance. One day I decided to try it differently. I decided to engage my mindfulness practice.

From that moment on, my daily encounters with the vendor became playful and even enjoyable. I found I was negotiating mindfully, with my attention both on the banter between the vendor and me and on my own internal emotions, judgments, and physical sensations. I began to notice what part of the bartering process was causing me to tense up, what part to relax. I began to see how my judgments and perhaps a feeling of vulnerability were affecting my skill in building a relationship with the vendor. I even began to notice that my overall comfort and discomfort with the process was more related to the mood I was in when I walked into the market than it was to the bartering process itself!

One day, my mindfulness practice moved me right into being able to put myself in the vendor's shoes. I began to wonder whether there might not be more going on for him than just making a good deal. I noticed him smiling more, and that he had quite a sense of humor. It was actually kind of fun to relate to him this way.

As one of the cornerstones of Personal Leadership, mindfulness means attending to our internal environment, to our external environment, and to the interaction between the two, all at the same time. Just as Sheila was doing, it means engaging all of our senses out in the world—sight, sound, smell, touch, taste, and any others we can call on. It means engaging all the stimuli within us—thoughts, emotions, physical sensations. And it means paying attention to the relationship between these two realms, the external and the internal, and how sensory input in one arena speaks to and influences sensory input in the other.

Does this sound like a difficult task? Perhaps, but well worth it; the journey into mindfulness is an endlessly fascinating journey.

The purpose is to free ourselves from
powerful self-defeating emotional habits.

Mindfulness: Our Full Intelligence

And it turns out that when we are paying attention in this way, we are paying attention to the full scope of our intelligence.

Until relatively recently, western science taught that our intelligence was localized, either in our brain or in the DNA inside each of our cells. Michael Hyland explains in his article, "The Intelligent Body and Its Discontents" in *Journal of Health Psychology*, that while the brain was considered intelligent, the body overall was considered stupid. That began to change by the late 1980s as new research began to paint a dramatically different picture. Dr. Deepak Chopra reviewed that early research in his book *Quantum Healing*. Some 20 years later, Andrew Amour published the e-book *Neurocardiology* on the Institute of HeartMath website. In it, he presented the complex interrelationship we now understand exists between our brain, our heart, and our immune, endocrine, and nervous systems.

Whereas we once thought our brain sent impulses in straight lines via our nervous system, we now know that intelligence actually circulates throughout the body's entire inner network. Our mind-body intelligence is an intricate play of thoughts, emotions, sensations, chemicals, heart rhythms, and energy vibration. As we attend to our internal environment, to our external environment, and to the interaction between the two, we access this full intelligence.

A well-seasoned firefighter once told us of an inner sense of direction, a mind-body communication that guides what she does. For her and her colleagues, very understandably, fear is a common emotion. However, literally in the middle of a burning building, they can tell the difference between normal human fear and fear being driven by a deeper intelligence. The first fear, the normal human fear, is one they are trained to ignore no matter how strongly it is yelling at them to get out. The second fear, the mind-body fear, is one they know to listen to. It arises out of a mindful attention the firefighter holds towards (a) her judgments, her emotions, and her physical sensations; (b) her colleagues, civilians on the scene, and the rapidly shifting conditions of the fire she is fighting; and (c) how her internal experience changes as she does what she is trained to do.

The quality of intelligence required in new and unfamiliar situations is not unlike the intelligence on which our firefighter depends for her life. We, too, need to be effective in a time of uncertainty, complexity, and in a continually shifting landscape.

> *When we are paying attention in this way, we are*
> *paying attention to the full scope of our intelligence.*

Mindfulness: Ringing the Bell

One of the best known and well-loved instructors of mindfulness practice in a Buddhist tradition is the respected Vietnamese teacher

Thich Nhat Hanh. Based on his teachings, a literal "bell of mindfulness" rings in many personal development retreats. When it rings, all participants simply stop whatever they are doing to intentionally take deep breaths and pay absolute attention to what is going on around them and inside them. After completing the retreat, participants are encouraged to take the practice home: a ringing telephone, a honking horn, or any other common yet unplanned sounds can be used to help them remember to pay attention to both their outer and inner environments.

Practicing Mindfulness

by Barbara

About 15 years ago, I was transitioning from one job to another and decided to give myself a 10 week retreat in between. It was an important time full of reflection and emerging insight.

Just before I left the retreat center, one of the practitioners there recommended that when I get home I do something like move the silverware from one drawer in the kitchen to another. The idea was to create a momentary shock by not finding the silverware where habit dictated it should be. This would spring me into a more mindful state. I was skeptical, but even so, I moved the silverware around when I got home. It really did help. Each time the silverware wasn't where I thought it would be, I stopped, took a breath, and brought my attention fully present.

A ringing bell, silverware in an unexpected drawer—these are tricks to help us remember to open the door to our full attention in the midst of a busy life.

Another is to pretend that the situation we're in or the person we're encountering is completely new to us, no matter how familiar the moment already feels. For example, next time you walk out your front door, pretend you're doing it for the very first time. What sound does the door make? How does it feel when the outside air meets the inside air right there by your face? What do you see first as you look out? What internal experience—anticipation, trepidation—do you notice as you contemplate closely the world outside?

Take it a step further: pretend you've never actually opened a door before. Really be present, a full-body, multisensory presence, to the experience of opening a door. How do you grip the door handle? How much pressure do you exert on the door so that it opens? What kind of physical tension is generated in your body? What kind of dance step do you do with your feet to get out of the way of the opening door? What other questions can you ask yourself?

When a person or situation is familiar, we may indeed need to pretend to look and see in a new way.

INTERNATIONAL STUDENT ADVISING

by Mark

I've been working with international students for more than six years. By the third or fourth year, I'd heard every single story possible, every single problem, every single question. As soon as a new student started to speak, I could tell where she was going and what her issue was going to be. There was nothing new. Personal Leadership's emphasis on mindfulness has helped me transform my work. Rather than being tired of the same-old, same-old, I'm waking up to the new beginning in every interaction with every student. At first it felt like pretending, but the more I do this, the more I discover that every interaction really *is* new. It's not pretend; it's presence.

Pretending certainly isn't necessary when we find ourselves in a situation that is very different from any we have ever encountered before, or when we are interacting with someone who is unlike anyone we have ever met before. As we live or work in cultural environments different from our own, everything we encounter can serve to ring the bell of mindfulness. As Ellen Langer says in *The Power of Mindful Learning*, "diversity provokes mindfulness" (p. 98).

A ringing telephone, a honking horn,
or any other common yet unplanned sounds
can be used to help us remember to pay attention
to both our outer and inner environments.

Creativity

Creativity is Personal Leadership's second principle. Along with mindfulness, it forms the foundation for the Personal Leadership methodology.

Creativity: Being the Artist of Our Own Life

"Creativity" is a word that used to be reserved for people involved in the creative arts: painters, dancers, and poets. That's changed over the years, as popular culture has come to understand that everything we do can be done as a creative act whether we're negotiating a deal, manufacturing widgets, raising children, planting a garden, teaching a class, or serving a meal.

This shift in understanding what it means to be creative is embedded in Personal Leadership, too. Personal Leadership fundamentally assumes that each of us is the artist of his or her own life, whether or not we ever pick up a paintbrush or put on dancing shoes. In the context of Personal Leadership, this has the very practical consequence of positioning us as choice-making creatures.

RAINY DAYS

by Barbara

I live in Seattle, in the Pacific Northwest of the United States, and it rains a lot here. When I first moved to Seattle, my sisters teased me about moving to such a wet part of the world by quoting something they'd seen on a T-shirt: "Seattle rain festival, January 1st to December 31st."

Perhaps not surprisingly, the local weather forecasters are a bit obsessed with whether or not it's going to rain. When it is, which is often, it's very common to hear them warn of a miserable day ahead. One day I realized the implications of what they were saying: rain equaled misery.

I realized that if I let the weather dictate the quality of my day, then I would have relatively few joyous days in Seattle. I realized that it's all about choice— whatever anyone says or does "to" me, whatever the "weather," I choose how I experience the events and how I respond.

When we accept ourselves as the creators of whatever it is that we're experiencing, we have a choice as to how we will respond to any situation or circumstance presented to us. We never have to default to being a victim however great the temptation may be.

And the temptation may at times be very great indeed. How is it possible, any caring person is likely to ask, for people to consider themselves creators in the face of the truly awful things that happen? What about when we find ourselves the victims of oppressive systems or abusive relationships, when homes and lives are lost by war or famine or natural disaster? Experiences such as these are of such a different order of magnitude that it may seem offensive to even consider them in the same breath as the experience of a rainy day. And yet, Personal Leadership suggests that the difference is, indeed, of magnitude, not of fundamental principle.

Viktor Frankl has become a very famous example of someone who was able to live his life with this absolute kind of personal leadership, even in the face of the truly terrible. In his classic book, *Man's Search for Meaning*, he writes about how choosing with intention the ways in which he would emotionally respond to being in a Nazi concentration camp allowed him to survive horrific circumstances that would otherwise have destroyed him. He was able to maintain himself as the creator of his own experience: he made it his choice whether to love or hate, his choice to find meaning and renewed purpose.

The choice is very much the same, although thankfully not so extreme, when we're faced with the challenges of living in a multicultural neighborhood or working on a multicultural team. Will we be open to the unfamiliar or shut down? Will we engage differences as a creative resource and enhance the possibilities that exist for everyone?

To even begin to do what Frankl did, we must accept that our attitudes, our emotions, our thoughts, in fact everything that we experience about another person or a particular situation, arises from within us. What arises is certainly a response to external stimuli, but external stimuli aren't responsible for what arises. What arises is a reflection of who we are, a "push back" of what we care about and of what we believe. The more we take responsibility for what arises from within us, the more choice we have about how we'll respond to situations that fill us with uncertainty and to people who offend us, or who are offended by us. When we engage the world in this way, as the creators of our own experience, we're less influenced by our immediate reaction to external stimuli. Influenced instead by intention and purpose, we increase our likelihood of responding to others with competence as well as with integrity and authenticity.

What arises within us is
certainly a response to external stimuli,
but external stimuli aren't responsible for what arises.

Creativity: Tailoring Our Responses

In the context of Personal Leadership, creativity also means tailoring a response specifically for the particular dynamics of the situation in which we find ourselves.

Even those of us who think things through ahead of time can't possibly plan for all eventualities. It's impossible to plan an exact response to a given situation before actually being in the situation. It's impossible to know ahead of time what the specific dynamics will be when we meet someone from a different cultural background, find ourselves in a new and unfamiliar location, start a new project. No matter the quality or extent of our expertise, we can't completely plan a response and expect it to be the best response. The best response can only emerge from an intricately balanced combination of our past learning and our current creativity. The best response depends on our capacity to leverage the creative potential inherent in the new experience itself.

In other words, you can't *plan* to be creative, you simply *are* creative. What we *can* do ahead of time is learn to open the floodgates through which creativity can then flow.

What we mean by creativity is no less than the uprising of life energy from deep within. It is the source of inspiration and insight. It's a kinesthetic experience, a physical vibration of alignment and aliveness. It's what makes our hearts swell when we see a newborn smile for the first time or when we hear a glorious piece of music. It is what pumps our blood and heals our wounds and moves our limbs in response to our desire.

Creativity is the key dynamic, along with mindfulness, that helps us to be competent when we live and work in the midst of difference or the new and unfamiliar.

> *Creativity means tailoring a response*
> *specifically for the particular dynamics*
> *of the situation in which we find ourselves.*

Creativity: Cultivating Our Connection

One of the biggest barriers to creativity—and therefore to being effective when confronted with an unfamiliar person, place, or project—is "identification." By this we mean being so closely invested in our beliefs and our interpretations of things that we are them and they are us; literally, our identity is dependent on them and there is no separation between us. When we are enmeshed in that way, there is no room for other perspectives and choices. And when there is no room for other perspectives and choices, there is no creative space.

If you want to get *out* of identification, one of the best ways is to get *into* "not knowing." Not knowing can turn out to be the best friend we have, even though we may be used to thinking of it as our worst enemy.

Typically, to help calm ourselves in the face of the unfamiliar, to relieve discomfort and anxiety, we try to get things figured out as soon as we can. We don't like being challenged by situations that require us to hold contradictions, to stand squarely in the middle of opposing values, judgments, and emotions. In a flash we find ourselves choosing sides (any side!), just to get rid of the sensations of discomfort. This kind of closing down to not knowing very easily blocks our potential for creative responses.

As distasteful as we may find the dis-ease of not knowing, we need to be honest about the price we are paying when we take the nearest road to release. If we hold tightly to our ideas about what will happen in our next business meeting, international relocation, or conversation with a friend, we constrain our options.

It is possible, instead, to cultivate a kind of openness towards not knowing that can help us connect to our deepest creative resources.

If there is one thing that creative individuals have in common, it is curiosity and the willingness to follow curiosity into inquiry. Artists and scientists attest to the power of wonder, of wandering around in chaos, sure that someday, if they just keep asking the questions, sense and direction will emerge. Their practice is inquiry. Inquiry is the doorstop that holds open the invitation to something new.

DINNER WITH THE VICE PRESIDENT

by Sheila

I had a dinner meeting with the Japanese vice president of a large steel manufacturing plant. We met at an appointed time near Shinjuku station in the heart of Tokyo. After greetings, he asked me if I had anywhere I would like to go for dinner. I was delighted with his question for I had several favorite places in the area. I was about to suggest one when something stopped me. I paused, took a breath and paused again. I asked myself what I should say, and suddenly I knew that my answer in fact needed to be a question. "Oh, I am sure you know this area much better than I do, so surely you have a place in mind?" As it turned out, he had made reservations at a nearby restaurant. What would have happened if I had suggested a restaurant? No doubt, we would have gone there and at some point early on he would have excused himself and canceled his reservation at the other restaurant. I would have never known, yet the consequences of my cultural faux pas might have haunted me for years in this relationship.

Only because Sheila was willing to not know and to follow curiosity into inquiry was she able to proceed in a culturally appropriate way with the Japanese vice president. Her experience reinforces the very important point that expertise and competence are not the same thing. Sheila had extensive expertise in Japanese culture, all of which would have been useless to her in this situation had she not stayed present to the given moment, noticed and become curious about her hesitation, and then literally asked herself what that hesitation was about.

"Expertise," says Gail Sher in *The Intuitive Writer*, "leaves no gaps, no questions, no quest.... Doubt leads to an entry point" (p. 4).

Ellen Langer, whom we first mentioned because of her work with mindfulness in education, conducted experiments on the effect of knowledge on creative performance. She describes this research in *The Power of Mindful Learning*. In each experiment, participants were asked to build a bridge over an imaginary river using small wooden blocks; the height of the bridge would determine the size of the ships that could pass underneath, so it was deemed that the higher the bridge, the better. Before being released to build the bridge, half the participants were briefly shown examples of how the blocks could be used to build something similar: a tall tower, a long but low bridge, and so on. The other participants were given no prior exposure to the bricks.

The results were dramatic. Ninety-two percent of the first group, the one that had been primed and therefore had some expertise with the blocks, tended to use building formations similar to what they had previously experienced. Only 8% of the group that didn't have previous expertise used those particular formations. Moreover, the group with prior expertise came up with only two ways to build a bridge; the group with no prior expertise came up with 10.

Langer and her co-researcher had hypothesized that the group shown examples of how to use the blocks would be constrained in their future creative innovation with the blocks. And sure enough, when it came to building their bridge over the river, they focused on what they knew of past success rather than accessing the creative potential of the given moment. Although Langer doesn't discuss this in presenting the experiments, no doubt the second group, the one that came up with 10 ways to build the bridge, stayed in curiosity and inquiry. As Langer would say, "uncertainty creates the freedom to discover meaning" (p. 130).

Wendy Palmer, author of *The Intuitive Body*, is a master teacher who applies the principles of the martial art aikido to the practice of "conscious embodiment." She has said that when we are pushed to our edge by situations whose newness throws us off balance and into confusion, we can only carry on in the spirit of inquiry. The principles of mindfulness and creativity help us to do so.

> *If there is one thing that creative individuals*
> *have in common, it is curiosity and*
> *the willingness to follow curiosity into inquiry.*

Try This: Learning Through the Two Principles

Mindfulness:

Step One. Give heightened attention to your external environment.
- Take a moment and sit quietly; let your breath move in and out through your chest area as if you are breathing in and out through your heart.
- As you continue this way of breathing, look around you. See where you are: what are the colors and textures and shapes that surround you? Look for nuance: can you, for example, see different shades of green when you look at the leaves on a tree, or of blue when you look at a cloudless sky?
- As you continue this way of breathing, listen around you. What do you hear? Traffic, commercials on the radio, birdsong, people talking, wind in the trees, coffee perking, children laughing? Listen for nuance: can you, for example, hear various kinds of birds singing their different songs?
- As you continue this way of breathing, feel around you. What is the feeling of your clothing against your arm or leg? What kind of pressure do you feel at the meeting point of body to couch or

chair? What's the feeling of the air on your face? Feel for nuance: can you, for example, feel the difference in temperature of your skin out in the open and your skin protected under clothing?

Step Two. As you continue this way of breathing, go within. Place your attention fully inside your own body, on your internal environment.

- What are the sensations in your physical body? Where is there expansion, where contraction; where is there relaxation and ease, where tension or tightness? Feel for nuance: even within the expansion, where is there contraction; even within the contraction, where is there expansion?
- What emotions are present? What thoughts? Don't evaluate them, just simply notice. And notice the nuances: what shades of emotion are you experiencing; what shades of thought distinguish one from another?

Step Three. Make it your intention to mindfully experience the next few moments.

- Give your full attention to some aspect of your surroundings or listen fully to a sound you can easily hear.
- At the same time, let the rhythm of your heart-centered breathing anchor your attention into the full field of sensations within your body.
- Can you begin to sense that you are in two places at the same time?
- As this begins to happen, notice the relationship between what you are seeing and hearing on the outside and the emotions, sensations and thoughts on the inside.

Creativity:

Step Four. As you continue holding this quality of both internal and external mindfulness, look around you. Wherever you are as you're reading this, pick up three small objects nearby.

- For example, you might choose paperweights and pencil holders if you are at your desk, objects off your coffee table if you're in your living room, leaves and twigs and whatever else strikes your fancy if you are outside.

- As you choose your three things, notice what calls you specifically to them rather than to something else. What's the sensation or the draw that has you choosing them? Where in your body does that sensation originate? What does it feel like?

- Now arrange these three things in relationship to one another. Again, notice the sensation within yourself that lets you know when your arrangement is pleasing to you or when it needs adjustment. Where in your body does the sensation originate? What is its quality?

Ongoing practice:

Step Five. Practice mindfulness and, as Robert Fritz recommends in *Creating*, create something new every day for five weeks.

- Start by giving yourself even as little as five minutes a day for mindfulness practice. When you first begin, it will probably be easier for you if you stop whatever else you're doing each time you engage this process. You may also find that it's easier for you to remember to practice mindfulness if you give yourself practice reminders.

- Merge your mindfulness and creativity explorations. What you create can be just about anything. It could be a meal or a cake, a flower arrangement, a report on a project for work, a braid in your daughter's hair, a song about your trip to class that day, a well-facilitated meeting, an album of photographs from a holiday, a letter to a friend, a sculpture using pipe cleaners or drinking straws, etc.

- However big or small, give yourself a part of every day when what you are doing is intentionally creating—just that, creating—and pay attention to how it feels.

- Remember to begin each process of creation with a few minutes of mindfulness practice, and to take that quality of mindfulness into the whole creative process.

• When the five weeks are over, compare your life during these five mindful and creative weeks with your life otherwise. What's the difference?

To Summarize

The two principles of Personal Leadership are mindfulness and creativity.

- They are interactive and mutually sustaining.
- Mindfulness is a quality of presence that allows us to access the full scope of our intelligence: thoughts, feelings, and physical sensations.
- Creativity puts us at the center of our own life, as the artist of our own experience, able to tailor uniquely appropriate responses to each situation and encounter.
- Mindfulness and creativity are each made real in our lives when we engage our experiences from a position of openness and inquiry.

Part Two

THE SIX PRACTICES

The two principles of Personal Leadership are brought into real-life applications through Personal Leadership's six practices. In this section we introduce you to them. They are:

1. attending to judgment
2. attending to emotion
3. attending to physical sensation
4. cultivating stillness
5. engaging ambiguity
6. aligning with vision

These practices are independent practices. That is, there isn't any particular order to them and none is more or less important than any of the others. Just as with the two principles, however, they each inform the rest and all are mutually sustaining. The more you work with all six practices, the more you'll maximize your competence in the midst of difference and uncertainty.

Practices of Personal Leadership

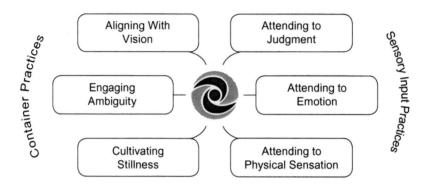

The first three practices in the list above, the ones that involve attending, are what we call the three "sensory input" practices. That is, these practices refer to the way we interface with the world: through our cognition (which manifests as judgment), through our emotions, and through our physical bodies. Our judgments, our emotions, and our physical sensations are how we know what kind of meaning we're making about the world around us; becoming attentive to them lets us take leadership of the kind of experience we're having. Becoming attentive to them simply means noticing them (mindfulness) and becoming curious and inquisitive about them (creativity).

The last three practices in the list above are what we call the three "container" practices. We call them this because they almost literally hold us, sustain us, as we attend to our judgments, emotions, and physical sensations. The container practices help keep us motivated, help us be attentive even when we'd rather just move forward on automatic pilot.

We'll now walk you through each practice, with one practice per chapter. We'll start each one with a short, basic description of the practice. We'll then briefly explain it, and share some stories. When you finish this section, you may still have uncertainty about what we mean by the practices, or what the practices actually look like in real life, or why the practices are so important that we've identified only six over all. Don't worry about it!

The best way to get to know the real meaning and the real power and value of the practices is to live your way into them. We only expect you to have a first-level understanding from reading each chapter. Your understanding will deepen as you read the rest of the book, with more and more stories showing the practices in application. Your understanding will really deepen, however, only as you start to explore the practices for yourself. You have to live these practices, not just think about them, if you want to get their full value.

The best way to get to know the real meaning
and the real power and value of the practices
is to live your way into them.

CHAPTER THREE

Practice: *Attending to Judgment*

Kidnapp'd tongue squirms loose
Out of the tight grip of head
Takes comfort in heart.

Automatic judgments prevent us from mindfully observing and creatively engaging what is going on in the present moment. Watch your thoughts. Examine your judgments, both positive and negative. Inquire about the sources and consequences of your judgments before you act on them.

Many people would say that one of the most important things we can do if we want to live and work effectively in situations of difference is to keep an open mind, not judge others, give people the benefit of the doubt. Do you agree?

If you think about it, this really does make sense. How can you meet someone halfway, how can you be effective with someone different from yourself, if you're busy judging them?

To Judge or Not to Judge (Is That the Question?)

Judgments are directly linked to our belief systems—personal, social, spiritual, cultural—about what is good and what is bad.

Whereas descriptions are based on relatively clear and measurable aspects, and interpretations relate to explanations, judgments assign positive or negative valuations.

Description	Interpretation	Judgment
He's 6'9" tall.	He's tall because his parents were tall.	He's the perfect height for playing basketball.
The water in the lake is 53F.	The cold temperature is a result of melting snow in the mountains.	The water is too cold for swimming.

It is because judgments are so subjective that they seem dangerous to people who care about navigating differences effectively. It's all too easy to judge something unfamiliar as bad simply because it is unfamiliar, and something else as good just because we know it. Not surprisingly, most of us quickly respond to any hint of this kind of judgment with a strong measure of defensiveness. It makes sense, then, doesn't it, that to navigate differences effectively we have to develop the capacity to be non-judgmental?

The tricky thing of course is that, being human, we can't actually be non-judgmental.

In *The Tree of Knowledge*, biologists Humberto Maturana and Francisco Varela wrote that, as biological beings, humans necessarily operate from habit and necessarily judge. Judgment is wired into us so that we can distinguish danger from safety. The best we can do with our judgments, as they suggest, is to recognize them, step back a bit, suspend them, inquire into them, and allow change. We cannot, however, get rid of them.

What the Personal Leadership practice of attending to judgment means is that we can be aware, at least to a point, of how we are always in the process of constructing our world by how we choose to experience it and evaluate it.

Confronting Prejudice

by Jin

I am an avid runner, and I planned to run every morning during my time at the conference. My friend Kareem knew this, and so introduced me to Adam, a blind man who also wanted to jog in the mornings. My first impulse was to say "No"; I am uncomfortable dealing with disability issues and especially with vision impairment.

Our run started out very tentatively. I was not sure how to lead him alongside the road with a foot-long bungee cord connecting us. It felt awkward. The morning traffic on the main road added to my anxiety.

As we entered a two-mile stretch in a quiet neighborhood, I began to relax more, was able to run more freely, and I was less and less concerned about leading with the cord. We started to talk, and I discovered that he is a third generation Japanese-American (I'm an American-influenced Japanese), a leadership and diversity trainer (I do leadership development with international students), had almost come to a conference at the university where I work, and runs marathons (as do I).

Look at all of these commonalities that I would not have discovered had I not agreed to run with him!

It then occurred to me that perhaps the reason for my discomfort with blind people is that their blindness creates such a judgment in me around our difference that I automatically disconnect myself from them. I shared this with Adam, who generously responded that my blind spot (yes, pun intended) is understandable given that I am Japanese born and raised; people with disabilities in Japan are segregated and not visible in our society.

It was a painful reminder of how social belief systems can limit opportunities for interaction and, as in my case here, create a hot spot of judgment and discomfort.

In order to navigate differences effectively we don't need to try to do the impossible, to *not* judge as we might traditionally be advised.

Instead, we need to embrace the potential bestowed by this human tendency. We need to develop a new relationship with judgment. This new relationship centers on developing the skill of discernment, by which we mean "clear seeing."

It's all too easy to judge something unfamiliar as bad
simply because it is unfamiliar,
and something else as good just because we know it.

Mindful Judgments

As we pay more attention to our judgments, we discover that they are not all the same. There is a difference between making a mind*less* judgment and a mind*ful* judgment.

A mindless judgment is so loaded with either positive or negative valuations that we are starstruck on the one hand and blinded on the other. Either way, our sight is clouded.

A mindful judgment is one that evaluates and at the same time notices the very act of judging: we judge and at the same time we take a learning orientation toward the judgment. We examine the sources of our judgments. We examine the effects of the judgments on us, on our interactions, and on the goals we wish to accomplish. We discern whether our judgments encourage us to engage with difference creatively or whether they encourage us to shut down. We ultimately make decisions and take action with greater clarity as we break through the confines of our automatic, mindless evaluations.

DIVERSITY DIALOGUE

by Sheila

There were about 15 people in the group. They were of different nationalities and of different U.S. ethnic and racial groups. One young European-American man, Ken, made a strongly negative evaluative statement about women. All conversation stopped with a jolt and the women in the room glared at him. The atmosphere was immediately heated and many of us began, literally, to sweat. As a facilitator, I was beginning to think about the options I could take if all the women in the room went after Ken.

Then, after a long silence, an African-American woman, Karen, asked Ken to think about and then to tell us the assumptions upon which his opinion was based. He did. She asked him where in his life these had come from. He explored these with the group. All of us were very engaged, rather than paralyzed. The courage, of both Karen and Ken, touched all of us. The door opened for others—not to agree with him but to powerfully share the kinds of experiences that had shaped our opinions about gender and race. The sense of community and mutual commitment to learning and growth that developed among those 15 people was enormously profound.

Becoming mindful of our judgments is a transformative act. It allows us to explore rather than to confront, and opens the door for deeper experience.

It would be easy to say that Ken was pretty foolish to speak out the way he did, to make an offensive statement about women in a room full of women without realizing that they'd likely jump on him for it. From a Personal Leadership perspective, however, that's missing the point. Even if Ken hadn't voiced his judgment when he had it, he still would have had it. It would still have influenced his subsequent perceptions and behaviors. Attending to judgment is about much more than simply keeping our judgments to ourselves. Whether we ever speak them out loud or not, and certainly there's no need to do so, we need to recognize them. We need to unpack the learning that our judgments offer us about ourselves if we want to be effective in times of change and in situations of difference.

Becoming mindful of our judgments
is a transformative act.
It allows us to explore rather than to confront,
and opens the door for deeper experience.

Judgments as Mirrors

Our judgments can function as mirrors, reflecting back to us our own values and beliefs. Muneo Yoshikawa calls this process "mirror-reflecting perception." His chapter, "Cross-Cultural Adaptation and Perceptual Development" in the book *Cross-Cultural Adaptation*, suggests that, when we're willing to look at them closely, our judgments can tell us a lot about ourselves and about our social and cultural conditioning. Inquiring in this way into the forces behind our judgments allows us to disengage from them, at least to some degree, and gives us much greater flexibility of response.

Rather than attempting not to judge, and failing, we can build a new relationship with judgment that encourages us to use our judgments as windows to new learning and clear direction.

Working with judgments comes down to choice, as does so much in the practice of Personal Leadership. One powerful choice is to engage each judgment with a "reframe." We can choose to look for what is valuable, what we appreciate, what gives us a sense of connection. This is particularly important with our negative judgments, which, unlike our positive ones, often spiral us into a sense of separation from the other people involved or from the situation itself. Looking for what we appreciate gives us a way to reconnect across the negativity of our judgment and, thus, motivates us to engage the judgment as a mirror into mindfulness.

In the story that follows, Hyun-Ju did exactly this with the negative judgment she was having about her professor's competence. She used it as a mirror to better understand her assumptions and beliefs about appropriate teaching styles, and then looked for the opportunity being presented as a way to stay committed to the learning process.

TEACHING STYLES

by Hyun-Ju

As an international student newly arrived in the United States, I was furious after my first two literature classes in the small liberal arts college I was attending in Illinois. I asked for an appointment with the chair of my department. I bitterly told her that I was so disappointed because I had made a terrible mistake in coming to this school and was wasting the little money my parents had. The chair asked me to tell her about the classes so far. I told her that the professor knew nothing! He was only asking questions and rarely giving his own opinion or facts. He was not teaching us anything and only asking other students for their opinion. I was learning absolutely nothing.

The chair of my department suggested I go to talk to the counselors in the international student office. I did not do this for a month because I was embarrassed but finally I was too upset and I could not study. I met other students at the international student office who felt the same way I did when they first came to this school. I was not alone! But I saw that they had changed. Some of them said that now they actually liked the class discussion; they said it made them think more. They said it was teaching them to make their own opinions and be more critical. To be honest, I realized I was not used to voicing my own opinions without more guidance from the professor. I decided that if I was here in America I needed to learn all I could, even if it was about how to learn in an American style. So, I started to see what good this way of teaching could do for me. I started telling myself that the professor knew what he was doing, and I found that I could sometimes relax. I began to actually enjoy the debate. I was surprised; it did make me think more, and more clearly.

Looking for positive value in the person or situation we are negatively judging helps us break through the narrow focus our judgments impose. We become able to see the rest of the story. That is the ultimate purpose, whatever the quality of our judgments; whether they be positive or negative, we want to be able to see, or at least free ourselves up to imagine, the parts of the story that our judgments otherwise hide from us. That then frees up the creative potential in the situation, much as it did for Hyun-Ju as she began to enjoy her professor's interactive teaching style.

The internal space this creates is necessary before we can clearly determine what action we need to take. We may end up taking essentially the same action, but, before, we would have been doing so mindlessly. Now, instead of being lost in the chaos of our judgments, we lead ourselves through it. As a result we connect more easily with our larger intentions, vision, and purpose, and thus strengthen our decision-making ability. Like Hyun-Ju, we are able to see options and creative opportunities that were not available before. As chaos theoreticians have pointed out, there is order in chaos: seeing the patterns in the waterfall is largely a matter of how close or far away the observer is standing and where the observer chooses to look. Attending to judgment is about bringing perspective to chaos by stepping back into reflection so that we can see the full picture.

We want to be able to see, or at least free ourselves up to imagine, the parts of the story that our judgments otherwise hide from us.

Try This: Learning Through Judgment

Step One. Commit to paying attention to the judgments you make.
- Choose a block of time—at least 15 or 20 minutes—while you are doing something that is important to you.
- Notice the judgments, both positive and negative, that come up as you do whatever you are doing. They may come quickly, one right after the other, so be sure to pay close attention.
- Write them down as you notice them, and then continue with whatever you're doing.

Step Two. Become curious about both the target and the effect of your judgments. Look back on the judgments you made and use the following questions to explore them.
 Target:
- How many of the judgments you made were about others, how many about yourself?
- How many were about what you were actually doing right then and there?
- How many were about something that happened in the past or that you imagine will happen in the future?
- How many had a positive valuation, how many a negative?

Effect:
- How did your judgments affect your current energy? Did they give more energy or deplete you? Did the effect differ for positive versus negative judgments?
- How did your judgments affect your curiosity? Did they open you up to wonderment or shut you down?
- Did the judgments make you more or less skillful at what you were doing?
- Did the judgments make what you were doing more or less enjoyable?

Step Three. Relax and reflect.
- What patterns do you see in what you targeted with your judgments, in whether they were positive or negative, and in what effect those judgments had on you?
- What difference can you notice in the quality of your judgments and their effects, now that you're more mindful of them?

To Summarize

- It's impossible to not judge.
- Judgments can be either positive or negative; both cloud our ability to see clearly. Negative judgments, however, also create a quality of separation that positive judgments typically do not.
- When we use our judgments as a mirror, they tell us about ourselves and most especially about our expectations and assumptions.
- Focusing on what we appreciate in the person or situation we are negatively judging can strengthen our resolve to turn around and learn through our judgments, to transform them from mindless to mindful.
- As we disconnect from our automatic judgments, we can creatively reframe them to find the opportunity inherent in them.

CHAPTER FOUR

Practice: Attending to Emotion

Oh, worlds to explore
A thousand places to go
Right here, inside of me!

Emotion paradoxically both blocks and offers an opportunity to learn about the specific situation or encounter. Rather than engage or suppress your emotion, move into the neutral perspective of witness and observe yourself. Follow the emotion to its source, and to the insight it has to offer. Notice how your emotion changes.

Emotions are a marvelous and fascinating dimension of human experience. They bring drama, depth, and passion to our lives. Living without emotion would be like living in a house without any color.

Imagine if everything in your home—the paint on the walls, the carpets on the floor, the furniture, the books, the art, every single thing—were all the same beige color. No flashes of brilliant orange or vivid green, no heated red or sparkling blue or shining yellow. Not even any variations on the theme; no off-white or grey or shades of brown and black to help you distinguish one item from the next.

The Roller Coaster of Life

Emotions, like color, bring texture and dimension to our lives. Their powerful, driving force can rise up out of nowhere, in a flash, pushing us in an instant from a joyful high to a fearful low. Our emotions are like our very own built-in roller coaster, pushing and pulling, lifting and dropping, often with barely a moment's notice, as they lead us up one side of life and down the other.

What fuels our emotional roller coasters? Why is it that the very same thing that may make one person angry may make another person laugh?

As with automatic judgments, emotions arise from subjective experience. They often come upon us so fast that they stimulate us to action even before we've had time to consider whether it's the right action for the particular situation.

AT THE COFFEE SHOP

by Barbara

I was at a coffee shop with my friend Andrew when another friend of mine, Ruth, came in with a visitor from out of town. Ruth came over to introduce us to her guest, who then proceeded to talk quite awhile about someone we all knew, except for Andrew. He left to get something at the counter, and Ruth's guest kept on talking.

After quite awhile, Ruth and her guest moved to their own table, and Andrew returned. Sitting back down, he made a comment about how long Ruth's guest had stayed at the table. I laughed in acknowledgment of how talkative she had been. As I looked up at Andrew's face, however, I discovered that he wasn't laughing, that he was in fact very angry.

What I had experienced as tiresome but funny, Andrew had experienced as personally dismissive.

Who was right and who was wrong in the coffee shop that day? Was Barbara wrong to find the situation funny? Was Andrew wrong to get angry? Of course not; they were riding their respective roller coasters, the different trajectories of their emotional response to what on the surface looked like the same interaction. Both were influenced by their different histories and backgrounds.

One of the tricky things, of course, is the consequence to relationships when people have different emotional responses to the same event.

For Barbara and Andrew, building on a long history of relationship, it turned out to be relatively simple to negotiate through the personal and cultural differences that drove their needs and expectations. At other times and places, however, laughing about something when the other person finds it hurtful can break relationships, destroy contract negotiations, stop projects altogether.

As with judgments, therefore, the subjective nature of emotions might suggest that we should be "non-emotional" or, at least, that we shouldn't express the emotion we do have. After all, if we can't trust our emotions to be accurate reflections of the situation at hand, we shouldn't let our emotions drive what we think or say or do.

But of course, being non-emotional is as unrealistic as being non-judgmental. And, being emotional but deliberately suppressing it is also problematic, no matter how well-intentioned we may be in our desire to be sensitive to cultural differences.

Suppressing our emotion, you see, is not at all the same as taking leadership of it.

First of all, when we suppress our emotions, they don't go away. They are all still in there, driving our actions and perceptions. Indeed, when we suppress emotion it's like pushing molten lava back into the volcano: the pressure builds and builds, getting stronger than the original force. When it does erupt, it's usually at unexpected, and often unwelcome and inappropriate moments. And while the pressure is building in our internal volcano, we're doing damage to our stress levels, our blood pressure, our adrenal glands, and more. Numerous authors write about this, among them John Sarno in *The Divided Mind* and Esther Sternberg in *The Balance Within*.

The following story illustrates how easily emotion can be displaced. As you'll see, Sheila thought she knew why she was angry but, until she stopped to look at it directly, she was actually targeting the wrong source.

CULTURE SHOCK IN INDONESIA

by Sheila

Barbara and I were working in Indonesia on a fabulous project. Along with interesting work and a great client community, we were enjoying Indonesia itself, not least the chance to have Indonesian food at every meal.

About 10 days into our stay, I went off to join Barbara for a late breakfast in the hotel restaurant where we had agreed to meet to discuss the next phase of our work. Walking down the hall to the elevator, I felt disgusted at the thought of having chicken porridge yet again for breakfast. Looking out the window as I waited for the elevator to arrive, I felt revulsion at the thought of living in Indonesia and was glad I didn't.

Trying to order whole wheat toast for breakfast, I was infuriated that the waiter couldn't understand what I was asking for and was making no effort to meet my needs.

Observing my unusual behavior, Barbara asked me what was going on. As I prepared to launch into the trials of what some expats there call "having an Indo day," I paused. What was I feeling? I took a breath, and another breath, and realized I was upset about an e-mail from home that I had read before leaving to meet Barbara. What I was feeling had nothing to do with chicken porridge for breakfast (which I really like) or with being in Indonesia.

Becoming mindful of what was actually driving my emotion allowed me, in that instant in the restaurant, to reclaim my full presence for our work in Indonesia. We had a great planning session (and a good breakfast), and went on to implement a highly successful third phase of the contract. Just as importantly, I was later able to respond with presence to the e-mail from home.

Emotions, and the situations that stimulate them, offer information about what we care about, our core values and beliefs.

It's endlessly fascinating to treat our emotional responses to people and situations as a mirror: what does the mirror reflect back? Whether the reflection in the mirror is pleasant or unpleasant, the mirror transforms our emotional responses into a doorway, an opportunity to learn about ourselves in the context of a particular situation or experience.

TEAM TRAINING

by Barbara

I was co-training a seminar with someone I didn't know very well, who eventually started really getting on my nerves. I found myself feeling impatient and anxious each time it was her turn to lead the group. I asked myself why, and quickly realized that our training styles are very different. Mine is what I consider North American: friendly, highly interactive, and directive only in an indirect kind of way. For example, it's rare that I tell participants I think their contributions to the discussion are wrong. Instead, I'll find a way to weave their ideas into the meaning we're making together; I use their "wrong" ideas to shed light on the topic, to help define whatever value or applicability I think the ideas may have. My co-trainer's facilitation style, formed in Central Europe and the Balkans, is to just come out and say the idea is wrong, and usually in a way that feels too harsh to me.

Questioning my emotional reaction, I realized what a high value I place on creating a training room environment that inspires participant delight in learning. I want them excited and motivated even in the face of challenging content. I knew my co-trainer well enough to know that she wanted this for the participants too. I was able to relax, and to entertain the possibility that hers is just a different way of supporting the deeper purpose we both share. Indeed, over time, I've watched the way participants approach her during break, I've read the evaluation comments that pertain directly to her, and I see the high quality of relationship she and the participants create together.

When Barbara identified what it was she cared about most fundamentally, the more superficial differences in behavior became less important. She became able to give her co-trainer the space to do things differently because she knew that what really mattered was still being respected.

It's endlessly fascinating to treat our emotional responses
to people and situations as a mirror:
what does the mirror reflect back?

Witnessing Emotion

So what happens in more difficult circumstances, when our core values and commitments are being perhaps grossly challenged?

LISTENING TO THE FLIGHT ATTENDANT

by Barbara

As the plane began its descent into Seattle, the flight attendant began the usual announcement about putting things away for landing. I was barely listening until I heard her say something about there being members of the U.S. military onboard, on leave before returning to the war in Iraq. She asked if everyone would please join her in a round of applause to thank them for their efforts on our behalf.

I was outraged. I am a staunch opponent to that war. I am skeptical of the U.S. military industrial complex in the first place. I disagree with the way the United States is increasingly relying on military force for its foreign policy instead of working towards global justice. And I was outraged at her simplistic approach to showing support for the people our policy has put in horrific situations. I think it would be better to show support to the troops by actually equipping them properly, by adequately funding their medical needs upon their return, or, better yet, by addressing the ways our own consumption patterns are contributing to the rationale for fighting an unjust war.

All this was roiling through me at the same time that I was, in increasing emotional panic, wondering what to do. Was it safe not to applaud? Should I say something to the flight attendant on deplaning? How could I persuasively explain myself in the letter to the airline that I was starting to compose in my head?

Waiting for the luggage to arrive in baggage claim, I called a friend who also has a Personal Leadership practice. I ranted and raged, and she listened as I decompressed.

When I was ready, I turned myself to the question of why I care so much: my feelings of impotence in the face of the flight attendant's microphone monopoly were really my feelings of impotence in the face of U.S. foreign policy. My anger at the flight attendant's simplistic approach to addressing the war was really guilt at my inadequate involvement in trying to change U.S. foreign policy. As I began to deconstruct my emotion, to reclaim its origins within me, I noticed a soldier standing near the carousel waiting for the luggage to arrive. I felt an upwelling of compassion within me—for him, for the people of Iraq, for everyone being impacted by the war.

As you can see from this example, attending to emotion doesn't mean not getting angry. Or sad. Or happy. It just means that we don't stop there.

When we need to express our rage, we take responsibility for the way we do so. Barbara, for example, called someone with a Personal Leadership practice who could listen to her anger and despair without engaging it or getting into agreement with her about it. Barbara wasn't looking for someone who would tell her how right (or wrong) she was, only for someone who would ultimately expect her to detach from it, to use it as a mirror, and to discern from a place of self-awareness and personal responsibility what action to take, if any.

What Personal Leadership is aiming for is something we call "witnessing emotion."

Witnessing emotion means that we experience it without committing to it, fueling it, or denying it. Instead, we observe ourselves. We become curious about the emotion. We let it pass in and out just as we do one breath and then the next. The space that inevitably opens within us allows us to pay attention to the learning that lies just underneath whatever we've been feeling. From that place, we can find it in ourselves to remember that the other people too have core values driving them—core values that are equally important to them even if sometimes inexplicable to us. And from that place, whatever action we take, our emotion powers it instead of overpowering us.

Witnessing emotion means that we experience it
without committing to it, fueling it, or denying it.

Disentangling From Story

At the root of our ability to witness our emotions is our willingness to release the story we associate with them. In the examples above, Sheila was creating a good story about culture shock, Barbara first about teaching standards, and then about righteous rage.

Stories of this kind are very seductive, don't you find? We use them to justify our emotion and to rationalize our automatic reactions so that we don't have to take leadership of our own deep experience. Well-meaning friends and colleagues may help reinforce the story. Wanting to comfort us, they get into agreement: "Of course you don't want chicken porridge for breakfast, poor you, you're having a bad Indo day."

Disentangling from story can be easy, certainly easier than you may think. All you have to do is to notice that you're in a story and then take a breath. That's what Gordon did, in the example below.

STUDENT MISCOMMUNICATION

by Gordon

I used to work a lot with international students. One day, a newly arrived Korean student came up to me to ask a question. We discussed his situation and I answered his question, and so came to the end of the conversation—except he didn't leave.

I could tell he was waiting for something and was even getting a little bit uncomfortable, but I didn't know what or why. Finally, he lifted his head and looked at me directly and, with a tone of exasperation in his voice, said loudly "You're dismissed!"

I was shocked, and in an instant, I was angry. I felt totally insulted. Who was he, a student, to dismiss me, a member of the faculty! In the next instant, however, I took a breath.

Immediately I realized what had happened—he had been waiting for *me* to dismiss *him*. When I hadn't, he hadn't known how to free himself to leave except by declaring me dismissed. Suddenly the situation was funny to me, even though the student was clearly horrified at what he had done and I could still feel the adrenalin that anger had generated in my body.

Disentangling from story really can be that easy. Just notice the story and take a breath. And then another breath, and another breath and another breath.

Sometimes the story returns, over and over again. This kind of persistent story, the kind that returns even as we're exhaling from the last breath we took, may be why we tend to think disentangling from story is so hard to do. In the moment, however, all it takes is a breath. That's all that's required, every single time the persistent story stages a return: just take another breath. The point is to allow yourself to experience the emotion as a pure emotion, without any of the justification and rationalization of story.

When we're willing to experience emotion as pure emotion, we're willing to have the emotion become more intense at the same time as we're willing not to have the emotion at all.

Writing for the series *Quantum Consciousness*, Stephen Wolinsky notes that if we're attending to emotion in an attempt to get it to go away, then we're resisting the emotion; ultimately that means we're recreating it ever more solidly. When we're just as willing to not have the emotion as we are to have it, when we're free in both directions, then we're here, now, able to step mindfully and creatively through each moment of the intercultural experience with no emotional entanglements.

> *When we're just as willing to not have the emotion as we are to have it, when we're free in both directions, then we're here, now, able to step mindfully and creatively through each moment.*

Try This: Learning Through Emotion

Step One. Commit to paying attention to the emotions you have.
- Choose a block of time—at least 15 or 20 minutes—while you are doing something that is important to you.
- Notice the emotions, both positive and negative, that come up

as you do whatever you are doing. They may come quickly, one right after the other, so be sure to pay close attention.
- Write them down as you notice them, and then continue with whatever you're doing.

Step Two. Become curious about both the target and the effect of your emotions. Look back on the emotions you had and use the following questions to explore them.

Target:
- How many of the emotions you had were about others, how many about yourself?
- How many were about what you were actually doing right then and there?
- How many were about something that happened in the past or that you imagine will happen in the future?
- How many had a positive valuation, how many a negative?

Effect:
- How did your emotions affect your current energy? Did they give more energy or deplete you? Did the effect differ for positive versus negative emotions?
- How did your emotions affect your curiosity? Did they open you up to wonderment or shut you down?
- Did the emotions make you more or less skillful at what you were doing?
- Did the emotions make what you were doing more or less enjoyable?

Step Three. Relax and reflect.
- What patterns do you see in what you targeted with your emotions, in whether they were positive or negative, and in what effect those emotions had on you?
- What difference can you notice in the quality of your emotions and their effects, now that you're more mindful of them?

To Summarize

- Emotions are the roller coaster of life, offering depth and nuance to our experience.
- Personal Leadership is not about having no emotions, anymore than it's about having no judgments; it's about becoming mindful of them and a witness to them.
- The more we can step into a position of witnessing our emotions, the more we will be able to disengage from the story we tend to create around them.
- We can use emotions that are triggered in particular circumstances as a route to new understanding about what is important to us.

CHAPTER FIVE

Practice: Attending to Physical Sensation

It would be absurd
To rely on candlelight
When the sun shines bright.

The routines and patterns that we have developed to get along in the world live in our nervous systems and in our muscular patterns. Values and assumptions are embodied experiences and talk to us through physical sensation. Distinguish the knot in your shoulder, twist in your gut, expansion in your heart. Receive your body's guidance.

Let's begin with an experiment: remember a time when you were interacting with someone and it just wasn't going well. Where were you, who were you with, what happened? As you remember this time in your life, notice the physical sensations in your body. What are they? Where in your body are they located? What are their qualities?

Now remember a time when you were interacting with someone and it was going marvelously. Again, where were you, who were you with, what happened? As you remember the experience, notice the physical sensations you're experiencing. What are they? Where are they? What are their qualities?

Embodied Ethnocentrism

If you're like many of us, the two memories evoke quite different sensations in your body. Often, difficult experiences evoke a sense of internal contraction. Muscles tighten, especially in the neck and shoulders, in the stomach and lower back. Positive experiences, on the other hand, typically evoke a sense of expansion. The heart center opens up and the chest area releases and expands, muscles relax throughout the body, and there's an embodied sense of ease.

Can you imagine two people having these opposite responses to the same interaction? Read the next story for an example of exactly that.

SUCCESSFUL TRAINING EXERCISE

by Barbara

I was a participant in an intercultural communication workshop. We were given the assignment of taking six photos each, three of something that made us feel physically relaxed and three of something that made us feel physically tense. The photos were then developed and we reviewed them together in class.

We immediately noticed that there were two photos of the exact same thing: a bicycle chained to a bicycle stand. Same bicycle, same bicycle stand, both photos taken during the same time period. The only thing was, one participant, American, took the photo as demonstration of something that made her feel relaxed; the other participant, Dutch, took the photo to show something that made her feel tense.

We asked them to explain. The American was inspired by the bicycle as a symbol of our decreasing reliance on the automobile, and therefore on fossil fuels. She was particularly taken by the bicycle stand: so many people were by now riding bicycles that the university had installed stands specifically for them.

The Dutch woman had a very different reaction to the bicycle stand. For her it symbolized the danger of life in the United States, that even something as basic as a bicycle had to be locked up or it might be stolen. The image to her didn't demonstrate a decreasing reliance on the automobile, but an increasing alienation from social well-being.

As the two women discussed the photos they had taken, it became clear to everyone that culture is as much an embodied construct as it is an intellectual and emotional one. And like our judgments and emotions, it too is subjective.

Our cultural programming not only influences the way in which we judge our experiences and the emotions they stimulate, it also influences the ways our bodies respond physiologically. To what extent do we tighten up in a particular situation, and to what extent do we release and flow?

Ethnocentrism describes an assumption of the supremacy of our own worldview and the worldview of people who seem to be like us. Those of us who are committed to being effective in situations of difference, and in the midst of the new and unfamiliar, typically guard against ethnocentrism. That is, we know the human tendency is to be ethnocentric and so are careful to step outside of our own cultural and perceptual constructs to explore alternative possibilities. Many of us become adept at doing this with our judgments and even with our emotions, but forget about what Milton Bennett and Ida Castiglioni call our "embodied ethnocentrism." Their chapter, "Embodied Ethnocentrism and the Feeling of Culture" in the *Handbook of Intercultural Training*, discusses why it behooves professionals working in situations of difference to attend to their physical sensations.

Here's another example that illustrates embodied ethnocentrism.

TEAM BUILDING

by Keiko

About seven or eight years after first coming to study and work in the United States, I was selected to be part of a new multinational product team with two or three other members from Japan.

One day relatively early in the team's existence, in the context of a team process debrief, I told the others something of my own experience as a team member. I suspected my comment would confront some of the other members with their culturally insensitive behaviors, so I had debated with myself whether to raise the issues in this way or not. I would not have done so if this had been a Japanese team based in Japan. To do so would have been much too direct and brash. It would have broken the fragile harmony developing within the group and would have caused everyone, myself included, to be embarrassed.

I knew that our facilitator would lead us in a careful self-reflection, and that in a U.S. context the issues I was raising would be acceptable and even appreciated. Indeed, after a rather intense discussion that led us to new understandings about the ways in which we would work together, several team members thanked me for making possible what they saw as an improvement in the team's cohesiveness. As for me, however, I felt nauseous for several days afterwards when I contemplated what I had done.

Keiko's story is a wonderful illustration of embodied ethnocentrism. Despite her intellectual and emotional understanding of team development in a U.S. context, her physical body was responding as if she were still in Japan.

What do we do with experiences of embodied ethnocentrism? Just as with our judgments and our emotions, we practice attending to our physical sensations.

> *Our cultural programming not only influences
> the way in which we judge our experiences
> and the emotions they stimulate, it also influences
> the ways our bodies respond physiologically.*

The Canary in the Coal Mine

In the early days of coal mining, when there were many fewer safety regulations than there are today and less technology to help monitor conditions, miners used to take a small bird, a canary, down into the coal mines with them each shift. A canary is much more sensitive to carbon monoxide than a human, so a buildup of toxic fumes would affect the canary much more quickly than it would the miners. If the canary stopped singing, started to sway, had trouble breathing, or fell over dead, the miners knew to pay attention and get out of the mine.

For the canary to be able to warn the miners, however, they had to pay attention. It's the same thing for us with physical sensation.

LINGUISTIC PROTOCOL

by Barbara

I was in Europe for the first time since childhood, and especially pleased to be visiting France as a young adult professional. Having lived in France and in francophone Africa as a child, I was looking forward to meeting with French colleagues and having a chance to exercise my French language and French cultural competence. It was very much a voyage of homecoming for me, full of meaning on a deep level of personal identity, so of course I had a lot invested in the success of my experience and the quality of professional contacts I might make.

One afternoon, I went for a meeting with a senior colleague, a leader amongst the French members of my field. As we began our conversation, I automatically spoke with him in the formal, using *vous* as I had so long ago learned to do. And then suddenly, as if my informally inclined American self decided to come visit, I heard myself suggesting that we switch to the informal, that we start using *tu* instead of *vous* with one another.

Even as I spoke, I could feel my shoulders start to round, could feel the tension in my gut; even before I had a chance to think about what I was saying or see the look of shock on his face, my embodied French self was telling me I was making a mistake!

In the example above, Barbara's canary was a bit slow—or more to the point, her practice of attending to physical sensation in those days wasn't quite fast enough. This is true for many of us who grow up in the industrialized world, where intellectual and more recently even emotional intelligence have taken priority over physical intelligence.

With practice, however, we can all become skilled at interpreting our early guidance system, just as Gordon has in the example that follows.

DESIGNING A CLASS

by Gordon

I was sitting in a mandatory workshop. The agenda was on infusing modules about English as a Second Language (ESL) into our teacher education program. I knew, respected, and liked the outside facilitators.

As the program got underway, my colleagues (whom I also liked and respected) began making comments about how we should be infusing ESL into our classes: we should be doing this, we should be doing that. Some of the classes they were referring to were my classes. In my head, I started defending my current design: we *have* been doing that—and that, and that! Indeed, we already had a long history of bringing ESL experts (the very same experts who were teaching us now) to my classes!

I sat there silently defending my class and mentally arguing with my colleagues for quite a while. All of a sudden, I started to sneeze, nearly uncontrollably.

I've come to know over the years that this is a way my body has of telling me to pay attention. I sort of snapped back into being present, realized that I had been swept up in my judgments and emotions, and started to pay attention again to what the instructors were saying. In the space of just a few minutes, they said a couple of small things that started my creative juices flowing! I grabbed my pen and started writing. Within a few minutes, I had restructured my class, infusing into it a new way for my students to learn about ESL during the next year.

The new approach turned out to be a terrific way for my students to access understanding and empathy about the ESL learning process. Indeed, the change that I made in my curriculum has ultimately resulted in several of my students pursuing the state endorsement to teach ESL.

Over the years, Gordon has come to know that when he sneezes, it's his canary in the coal mine suggesting he pay attention.

In Sheila's story, below, her canary appeared in the form of a burst of physical sensation.

PROFESSIONAL OPPORTUNITY

by Sheila

I was in a copy shop one morning about two weeks before moving from Denver to Washington, DC. I noticed that the woman at the machine before me had left a page of material behind. I glanced at it, noticing that it was about a method for holding large-group planning events called Future Search. As I gave the page back to its owner, I introduced myself, telling her of my interest. We decided to meet so she could tell me about the method and her experiences with it. Our meeting turned out to be much more informative that I had ever imagined. As she spoke, my heart began to literally pound in my chest, my palms began to sweat and I was almost shaking. Sometimes all this was so distracting that I could hardly hear what she was saying. I felt an extreme sense of aliveness in my body.

A few days later, I moved to Washington. Very soon thereafter I had the opportunity to co-facilitate a large-group event using a process very much like Future Search. I was in heaven! I loved it, and I've now been using this type of approach for more than 10 years.

It turns out that what had seemed distracting during that first meeting in Denver was in fact the most important part of the communication: my body telling me that there was something life-changing going on for me.

Whether through sneezing, sweaty palms, or a pounding heart, whether through aches and pains, or through a sense of comfort and ease, our bodies let us know that something is going on and that we need to pay attention. When we do then pay attention, the wisdom of our bodies can communicate to us the answers that we need.

Research by such organizations as the Institute of HeartMath in Boulder Creek, California, is documenting that our brains and our hearts, indeed our brains and the whole of our physical bodies, are in ongoing communication. Each continuously influences the other's function. Our human version of the canary in the coal mine is a result of the physical body communicating with the brain: sending messages via nerve impulses, via hormones and chemical neurotransmitters, through blood pressure waves, and energetically through electromagnetic field interactions. To our conscious minds, these messages may seem to be in code. Attending to physical sensation is in part learning to decipher our bodies' own particular codes.

> *Our brains and our hearts, indeed our brains*
> *and the whole of our physical bodies,*
> *are in ongoing communication.*

Maximizing Performance

This new understanding of our physiology asserts that the quality of experience in our bodies affects our brain activity and, therefore, our performance. That means we can intentionally work with and through our bodies to improve our performance when we're confronted with the new and unfamiliar. Here's an example of Anna, a USAmerican expatriate spouse, doing exactly this.

LOST IN BRUSSELS

by Anna

I relocated to Brussels as an expatriate partner, my husband's company having transferred him and therefore the whole family. One day not long after arriving, my daughter and I got hopelessly lost on the way home from her school. We drove and drove, feeling more and more lost and frustrated. I didn't speak French or Flemish, and didn't even know which language to use in that part of Brussels. Suffice it to say, I was much too nervous to even try to ask anyone for help.

I was even starting to feel a bit panicked. Eventually I just couldn't take it anymore. I drove into a private cul-de-sac and got out. I was so frustrated—with myself, with Brussels' inadequate road signage, with my husband and his company—that all I could do with the intensity of the energy in my body was stomp and shout. My teenage daughter, unsure at first, eventually got out and joined me. The movement and sound soon had us feeling so ridiculous and so released that we were able to get back in the car and try again to find our way home. And now it was easy; we were home in less than 15 minutes.

Physical movement like this, driven by the body's need in and of the moment, is an enormously powerful tool. Whenever we need to clear out emotional energy like Anna's, or like Keiko's when she felt so nauseous after behaving in a non-Japanese way, authentic movement and authentic sound can help retune and realign our physical guidance system.

Here's another way to work with our bodies so that we can more effectively engage difficult moments.

TALKING WITH A STUDENT

by Barbara

We were on break from a class I was teaching and a student started to approach me. I really didn't want to talk, and suspected from the quality of her participation in class that she was going to be critical about something. So I stood up straight, planted my feet in a balanced way on the ground, and took a deep breath. I kept breathing as she approached and intentionally expanded my awareness, almost as though I were extending imaginary antennae. I could feel my energy calm and awaken, both at the same time. I found that I was easily able to be present to her concern and we in fact had a good interaction.

Do you notice in this example how emotion, judgment, and physical sensation are intimately connected? Barbara had some emotion (didn't want to talk), and she certainly had some judgment (a complaint is coming), so she intentionally adjusted her physical experience (stood straight, breathed deeply) so that she could be mindfully and creatively present to the situation. Rita did something similar in the story that follows.

CORPORATE TRAINING

by Rita

I was conducting a training program for one of my key corporate clients, and, as usual, had a multinational group of participants. I had decided to do things a little differently than I usually did, focusing less on technical issues and more on the interpersonal and intra-group dynamic.

I had barely finished introducing the next training segment when a participant challenged the value of the activity I had proposed. I felt a sudden flash of tension in my body, as if I were frozen in place. I stood up and walked over to the flip chart as an excuse for some movement, to release some of the tension and "defrost" myself. Even as I did so, in that split second with just those few steps, I found my center again. I proceeded to work with the participant's resistance. It resolved easily and the training segment ultimately helped the group articulate valuable issues of quality production.

This ability to adjust our physical experience to deepen our quality of mindfulness and our access to creativity is a very important part of Personal Leadership practice. Try it next time you find yourself in a difficult situation. If you're sitting, stand up; if you're standing, walk a few steps. If circumstances won't allow you to actually move, wiggle your shoulders and gently roll your hips. If you can't do even that, take a deep breath—we can at least always do that.

We can intentionally work with and through our bodies
to improve our performance
when we're confronted with the new and unfamiliar.

Keeping the Physical, Physical

Equally important is learning to simply receive your physical experience as physical experience. For most of us, that's probably unusual. We overlay our judgments and emotional stories on physical sensation all the time. Notice when you are rationalizing your physical experience, explaining it, for you may then be overlaying story on it.

SELF-DEFENSE PROGRAM

by Barbara

I used to assist in a full-force self-defense course. In a 23-hour training program, women were taught to defend themselves against a single unarmed attacker using incapacitating blows to the groin and knockout blows to the head. Some of the instructors, known as mugger instructors and dressed in protective clothing so they wouldn't get hurt, acted as the attackers against whom the women practiced their skills.

As a thank-you for helping out in what were very emotionally and physically intense classes, the assistants would get so-called reward muggings towards the end of each class. We knew they were coming, but never just when or from which mugger instructor. Each time I assisted, stretching before class so I would be ready to defend myself later that night, I found myself feeling fearful. One evening it struck me that what I was experiencing was energy moving in my body. I had been labeling it as fear because it made rational sense to me that I would be feeling scared, but what it really was, was just energy. As soon as I removed the label from the energy, my whole experience of it shifted. I wasn't feeling scared anymore, I was just experiencing energy in my body. Instead of tightening around it, I became able to receive it, expand with it, let it move on through with each intentional breath.

Removing the label from our physical experience means being willing to remove the judgment, the evaluations, the sense of significance, the story that we want to attach to it. As we said earlier, the same thing is true with emotion and judgment: removing the labels means being willing to simply experience the particular energy without trying to define what that energy may mean about us.

Remember Gordon's story about sneezing? What kind of story could he have overlaid on it? Perhaps "I must have some dust in my nose" or "Maybe I'm getting a cold." Instead of staying in that superficial realm, however, he let his physical sensation bring him to attention; if he hadn't, he might never have received the insights that led him to redesign his class.

Have you noticed one of the tricky things about this practice of attending to physical sensation? It's that sometimes there's only a subtle difference between receiving new information through our bodies and overlaying story on our physical sensation. It is often challenging to distinguish between new information and story. Yet we need to be sure we're not just making up a story to rationalize our experience and are in fact receiving new information. With practice, we can learn to free ourselves from our embodied ethnocentrism, from what our cultural programming would have us assume our physical sensations mean, and access the deeper wisdom that we call our "embodied knowing."

With practice, we can learn to access the deeper wisdom that we call our "embodied knowing."

Try This: Learning Through Physical Sensation

Step One. Commit to paying attention to your physical sensations.
- Choose a block of time—at least 15 or 20 minutes—while you are doing something that is important to you.
- Notice the physical sensations, both expanding and contracting, that come up as you do whatever you are doing. Be sure you pay attention to the physiological experience of your body, for example your heart rate and blood pressure, and not just to your emotion.
- Write down the physical sensations as you notice them, and then continue with whatever you're doing.

Step Two. Become curious about both the target and the effect of your physical sensations. Look back on the physiological responses you had and use the following questions to explore them.
    Target:
      - What kinds of stories did you notice yourself overlaying on top of the physical sensations? Did your stories focus on you or focus on others?
      - Did the stories you overlaid tend to leave you feeling expansive, alive, peaceful, joyful? How many brought forth feelings of being tired, contracted, limited?
      - How many were about something that happened in the past or that you imagine will happen in the future?

Effect:
- How did your stories affect your current energy? Did they give you more energy or deplete you?
- How did your stories affect your curiosity? Did they open you up to wonderment or shut you down?
- Did the stories make you more or less skillful at what you were doing?
- Did the stories make what you were doing more or less enjoyable?

Step Three. Relax and reflect.
- When you look at the targets of the stories you overlaid on your physical sensations, what patterns do you see? What patterns do you see in the effects those stories had on you?
- What difference can you notice in the quality of your physical experience as you become more mindful of the stories you tend to overlay on them?
- Learn to decode the messages from your body. Everyone's body is unique. What are the special ways your body speaks to you?

To Summarize

- Our physical sensations are our canary in the coal mine, our early warning system.
- Our physical sensations let us know when there is something going on and that we had better pay attention.
- As we learn to pay attention, we learn to decode what our bodies are trying to communicate to us.
- At the same time, we can purposefully align our bodies and use our physical awareness to help maximize our performance in unfamiliar or uncomfortable situations.
- As with emotion, the more we detach from story, the better!

CHAPTER SIX

Practice: Cultivating Stillness

My single heart's breath
Does nothing at all. Except
Craft the Universe.

Internal stillness makes possible a receptive space through which to receive information from our deep, creative connection. Quiet your mind. Disentangle internal experience from external circumstance. Breathe. Meditate through movement or sitting. Attend to what resonates as truth from deep within.

M ost of us live in a "sensational" world, a world rich with sensory stimulation. Everywhere we turn, there's another billboard to read, more road traffic to hear, people bumping into us, food cooking.... Our senses are bombarded with constant input. Airport departure lounges, at least in the United States, have televisions in every corner tuned to CNN. We listen to music as we work on the computer; we read a magazine or watch television as we work out in the gym.

Contemporary western society, wherever it occurs on the globe from London to Tokyo to Johannesburg to Sydney, has generated a culture of speed, pressure, productivity, and efficiency.

The Call to Stillness

Our internal experience is just as frenetic. Our judgments, our emotions, our physical sensations are constantly activated, a nonstop background of sensory experience forming the undercurrent of each moment. When something pops to the foreground, when we notice a judgment we're making perhaps, or an emotion we're feeling, and we layer it with explanatory or rationalizing story, we reinforce the sensation-full quality of our lives.

In the midst of all that is going on around us and within us, how are we to find a little bit of psychic open space?

In *Hare Brain and Tortoise Mind*, Guy Claxton suggests we can no longer distinguish between being well-informed and knowing a lot on the one hand and being wise and clever on the other. He notes that we are trapped in a single mode of thinking. It values being explicit, articulate, and deliberate, and emphasizes turning to the latest technology to find our answers when there's something we don't know. The research he presents in his book supports a different view: that it is sometimes more intelligent to be less busy and that we can be smarter when we slow down.

We need to slow down if we're to separate from automatic judgment, emotion, and physical sensation. We need open space if we're to hold up the figurative mirror and learn from what's reflected to us of our expectations, assumptions, and core values. Without slowing down and opening space, how are we ever to discern the right action for us to take in the midst of uncertainty or in situations of difference? How, like Kahlil in the example that follows, can we hope to keep our cool?

CAMPUS ASSAULT
_____

by Kahlil

As the person on the university campus responsible for student discipline, I am often in uncomfortable and sometimes even in dangerous situations. I've noticed that the way I respond in these moments has changed since I started my stillness practice. Somehow, I don't get all frenetic anymore; there's a kind of quiet place within me. I can call on a more calm energy that's there for me even in the midst of chaos.

A few days ago, a parent emotionally and physically assaulted me. It was shocking. The campus police have a new lieutenant whom I met for the first time as a result of this assault. He read my narrative of the event and then asked me about my martial arts training. I had no idea why he would ask such a thing, and I told him that I don't have any training like that. He then asked me if I was into meditation or something, saying that from my description of the interaction, I had to have had some kind of training that helped me keep my cool.

Kahlil was able to respond with skill to a dangerous situation in a way that impressed even a police officer who has daily experience observing people under stress. What was he doing?

He was cultivating a quiet or "still" mind. A still mind, with the frenetic background energy at rest, becomes a container that can hold all we experience, all our stories and our drives to automatic and habitual action, without overflowing. From that place, we can discern what needs to happen and what we're to do.

Here's a story from Sheila about exactly that.

APPRENTICESHIP IN JAPAN

by Sheila

I was six months into my apprenticeship with a Japanese potter. There were major issues and difficult feelings between us that I didn't really understand. Then I found out that she didn't want to extend my visa. I was getting kicked out! I didn't know the reason why, nor if there was any way to fix the mess I was in.

My Japanese was passable but certainly not good enough to discuss complicated emotional issues, so I asked a Japanese friend living nearby to help me have a conversation with my teacher. The evening before my teacher and I were to talk, I sat by myself in my room. I was sad and angry and confused all at the same time. I knew I had to become much more balanced before the conversation. I took a lot of deep breaths and honestly felt very resistant. I really just wanted to be angry with my teacher.

When I relaxed a bit more, very uncomfortable emotions surfaced in me, like huge amounts of embarrassment and humiliation. Me! I teach people how to be successful across cultures and I had made such a mess of things! I only felt dread about the upcoming conversation. There was enormous energy in my head and stomach, just swirling and swirling around. All I seemed able to do was go over and over the events, replaying conversations and searching for clues to explain what was going on. I couldn't get any clarity at all; I felt stuck and desperate for sleep.

Meditation was already a part of my daily life, so I decided to do the best I could to get quiet and still. I stretched and took a short walk in the dark, letting my steps bring my breathing to a smoother rhythm. Then I slowly sat down on the tatami. It was *so* intense. My brain was absolutely begging me to jump into the details all over again, trying to analyze and figure it all out. Every bit of my attention had to go to my breath.

I have no idea how long I sat there. I could hear the chirping of the crickets outside; slowly it became quieter on the inside too.

As I just sat there, I had a sudden realization. Much of my anxiety was tied to my desire to stay in Japan longer and to wondering how I could persuade my teacher to let me stay. If I could let go of this personal agenda, perhaps I could relax. So in that moment that's what I did: I told myself to just let it go, and immediately felt my body begin to deeply relax. Then the next message came through: don't focus on going or staying; just focus on really understanding what was going on for my teacher, just focus on listening as much as possible. My anxiety lifted. As I got ready for bed, I was totally surprised to realize that I was actually looking forward to the conversation.

My teacher and I had a pretty exhausting three-hour conversation the next day. Ultimately, I still had to leave my apprenticeship early, and the relationship was never repaired, but I learned an enormous amount about myself, about Japan, and about the power of cultivating stillness. Ultimately, I was able to pack my bags with a sense of completion and integration.

Sheila was so stuck in the stories she'd overlaid on her judgments, emotions, and physical sensations that she couldn't unplug from it all until she focused on getting to a place of internal stillness. That then allowed her to genuinely open up to whatever would result from the conversation the next day.

One of the key things here is that Sheila didn't keep trying to analyze what had happened, nor did she keep trying to plan her strategy for the upcoming conversation. The key to this was *not* thinking about the past or the future but, instead, to become quiet inside. By choosing to cultivate stillness, as difficult as it was, she stepped out of her usual ways of acting and reacting, and into creative options of listening and learning that, a moment before, were not imaginable.

We can all learn to do this. We can all learn to evoke this kind of internal spaciousness. Although the outcome was not what Sheila wanted, she was able to take her immediate next step with emotional balance and self-awareness.

> *Our judgments, our emotions, our physical*
> *sensations are constantly activated,*
> *a nonstop background of sensory experience*
> *forming the undercurrent of each moment.*

Stillness and Well-Being

Testimony over thousands of years from artists, scientists, and spiritual masters tells us what can happen when we become quiet inside. They speak of becoming clear about the inner source of their emotions, judgments, and sensations; about becoming more open to unimagined possibilities; about receiving insight for new direction; and about experiences of compassion, peace, and love.

For more than 30 years, western-trained scientists and adepts from mystic Christianity, Islam, Hinduism, and Buddhism have been exploring the physiological effects of spiritual practice. At the forefront of this movement, the Mind and Life Institute based in Boulder, Colorado has been fostering dialogue and research between modern science and the great living contemplative traditions as exemplified by Buddhism.

His Holiness the Dalai Lama of Tibet, actively involved in these dialogues from the beginning, spoke in 2005 to 14,000 neuroscientists in Washington, DC. His speech, reviewed in Arthur Zajonc's article

"Contemplative and Transformative Education," addressed bridging the gap between science and spirituality, the effects of Buddhist meditation, and ways to study these effects for the benefit of the scientific community.

Leading some of the research discussed by the Dalai Lama, Richard Davidson at the University of Wisconsin has been measuring the brain waves of Tibetan monks for many years. He presents his early work in "Alterations in Brain and Immune Function Produced by Mindfulness Meditation." His research shows how meditative states can actually change the functioning of the human brain. Positive thoughts and emotions such as happiness are associated with the left prefrontal cortex of the brain. Using functional magnetic resonance imaging (fMRI), Davidson found that meditating monks have especially high brain activity in this area. Davidson's research also shows that meditation can result in an improved immune system.

Still other research by Shauna Shapiro and her colleagues, presented in the article "Effects of Mindfulness-Based Stress Reduction on Medical and Pre-Medical Students," has shown that quieting the mind through mindfulness meditation can reduce overall psychological stress and anxiety.

The Institute of HeartMath is actively researching the power of the human heart. It turns out that the electromagnetic field of the heart is the most powerful rhythmic field produced in the body. This field envelops every cell, can be measured anywhere on the body and even up to several feet away, and is 5,000 times stronger than the electromagnetic field generated by the brain. When we cultivate a heart-centered meditative state, the rhythm becomes more coherent. This means the electrical frequencies generated by the heart, as measured on an electrocardiogram (EKG), are more ordered and harmonious. HeartMath researchers call this an internal coherence, an experience reported to feel like "amplified peace."

As we learn to maintain this heart-focused stillness, our brain's electrical activity begins to synchronize with our heart rhythms. Again in the language of HeartMath, this is called "heart-brain entrainment."

Using heart-based methods to self-generate states of coherence and entrainment can help us in many ways. It can improve our thinking abilities and give us more mental clarity for decision making. It can strengthen our immune system, reduce our blood pressure, relieve depression, and lessen prolonged anxiety and burnout. It can also increase our creativity, our capacity to care, our sense of connection to others, and our general sense of well-being. Clearly, all of this is helpful when we are facing the new and unfamiliar or are challenged by working with people very different from ourselves.

Meditative states can actually
change the functioning of the human brain.

The Emphasis on *Cultivating*

It is relatively easy to imagine cultivating a garden: we get out there, rain or shine, and we turn the soil and plant the seed and pull the weeds and harvest the bounty. It's an active, productive kind of pleasure.

It's much the same when we talk about cultivating a friendship: we get in touch and get together, we stick around to help in hard times and to celebrate in good, and we build a relationship that grows and flourishes across time. This too is an interactive, outcome-oriented kind of process. Is there then a bit of paradox in the idea of cultivating *stillness*?

We don't think so. When we're building and maintaining a stillness practice, we're doing all the same sorts of things. We're turning the soil and digging weeds. We're sticking around in good times and bad. We're building a relationship with our own deep wisdom and the source of our creative connection that grows and flourishes across time.

What we're cultivating, of course, is internal stillness and quiet. It has nothing to do with whether or not we're actually physically moving. We can be perfectly still with our bodies, but our brains can still be running around at great speed. Meditation practitioners call it "monkey mind" for a reason! Our thoughts and emotions and physical sensations pull us first in this direction and then in that direction, and a split second later in a third direction and then a fourth and fifth. The point is not what we're doing with our bodies in the physical dimension, but what's happening with the internal dimension of our experience.

When we think about the practice as a stilling of the brain rather than the body, we discover there are literally limitless ways to cultivate stillness.

Sitting meditation, in which we do, indeed, still the body, is one of the most traditional. Different forms invite us to focus on the breath moving in and out of our heart center, or the breath flowing across the space between our upper lip and our nostrils, or the breath moving into and out of our lower bellies, or the breath at a particular rhythm of inhale and exhale. Other forms direct us to focus on the light of a candle flame, or the sound of water flowing in a fountain. Yet others guide us to focus without engagement on whatever thoughts move through our minds, or on the repetition of a particular chant or statement or prayer. Each of these practices invites us to focus our attention into a very specified frame; everything else recedes from awareness and we receive the experience of the surrounding, still, spaciousness.

Spiritual traditions also offer numerous forms of moving meditation. Originally a practice based in Hinduism, yoga is now a contemporary form of secular meditation for people all over the world. Tai chi, qigong, circumnavigating a Buddhist stupa, and walking a labyrinth modeled on the one in Chartres Cathedral are all forms of moving meditation. We can also meditate on a dance floor or running track, in a martial arts studio or swimming pool, while gardening or knitting, while writing in our journals, even while taking a shower.

Buddhist practitioners emphasize not only sitting meditation and moving meditation but eating meditation and working meditation. Drawing on this perspective, we can think of "standing in line at the post office" meditation and "waiting for a friend at the restaurant" meditation.

AIRPORT MEDITATION

by Barbara

For some reason, perhaps because I spend a lot of time in them, I've developed what I think of as airport meditation. Airports can be such frenetic places, people hurrying to catch flights, people worrying about missing flights, people angry about canceled flights. As I stand in line at security, putting my lipstick in a clear plastic bag and preparing to take off my shoes, I feel my judgments start to rise.

When I practice airport meditation, I put my focus on my breath and let the space around my heart be soft. I keep my focus there as I put my computer through the screening process, browse my reading options at the bookstore, and negotiate the crowds of people at my gate.

Airport meditation doesn't always come easily to Barbara, and no doubt she sometimes forgets altogether that such a thing is even possible. That's why we call this *cultivating* stillness—it's an active process of commitment and practice.

In "Contemplative and Transformative Education," Zajonc suggests that the myriad forms of contemplative or stillness practice fall into two major categories. There are those that help us quiet our mind and become more discerning thinkers, and there are those that help us open our hearts and cultivate compassion. No matter which practices we choose, we amplify our sense of inner peace. It is this, he suggests, that gives us the inner resources to create peace in our multicultural world.

What we're cultivating, of course,
is internal stillness and quiet.
It has nothing to do with whether or not
we're actually, physically, moving.

Try This: Learning Through Stillness

Step One. Start a meditation practice.
- Pick a form of meditation—sitting, moving, eating, working— and practice daily.
- Set a timer to make it realistic for yourself. If it's most realistic for you to meditate for five minutes when you first wake up or for five minutes before you go to bed or for five minutes while you're on your lunch break, give yourself those five minutes.
- Experiment with a heart-centered meditation practice. Bring your focus to your heart center. Breathe as if you were breathing into and out of your heart.
- Try preceding each meditation with stream-of-consciousness journal writing. Clear the space for your meditation. Consider writing after meditation as well, especially if you're exploring a particular situation or experience. What new insights and understandings emerged from the stillness?
- When incessant, random thoughts seem to overwhelm your meditation, simply bring your attention back to your heart center. Instead of focusing on not thinking, focus on breathing into and out of your heart center.
- To help your focus stay with your breath into and out of your heart center, place your hand on your chest. Let the touch of your hand focus your embodied attention.
- Relax into your practice. Explore different traditions and disciplines until you find what suits you best. Commit to the expansion of your own internal stillness.

Step Two. Find your own airport meditation.
- Choose someplace you frequent such as the post office, your coffee shop, the grocery store.
- Experiment with cultivating stillness each time you're there. How does your experience of being in that place change as you open to the quiet within yourself?

Step Three. Relax and reflect.
- What value do you receive from your meditation practice? What do you notice about your stress levels, your energy levels, your levels of creativity?
- Notice what forms of meditation seems to serve you best: moving, sitting, eating, or working.

To Summarize

- The fast pace of the external world is a mirror of our madly rushing judgments, emotions, and physical sensations.
- Internal stillness strengthens our creativity, intelligence, resilience, and well-being.
- There are countless forms of meditative practice, from the deeply spiritual to the absolutely secular.
- The important thing is to find a stillness practice that serves us, and then to cultivate the stillness that it helps make possible.

CHAPTER SEVEN

Practice: Engaging Ambiguity

Red, rich tomato
Ripened gently in due time
What a tasty treat!

Change and difference create a time of uncertainty, of liminality, between what was and what will be. Embrace that time. Become comfortable with the sense of not knowing what to do. Allow possibilities to arise. Open yourself to inspiration and tap your infinite creativity for constructing appropriate responses.

Imagine that you've just moved to a new country, region, or city. Your boxes and bags are unpacked and you have a whole day stretching ahead of you, with no plans and nothing you must do. What now?

When We Don't Know What to Do

We can learn a lot about ourselves by observing what we decide to do when we don't, in fact, know what to do.

In this metaphorical new home of yours, what do you do? Do you pull out your guidebooks about the new city and curl up on the couch to read? Do you arrange a tour with a professional who knows the city well? Do you call the friend of a friend of a friend whose name you were given and suggest meeting for tea? Do you make clearly defined plans to go to the shops and the museums, have a meal, and be home by 3 p.m.? Do you grab a map and head out the door all on your own with no plans at all? Does your choice change if you look physically different from the people who live around you? Does it change depending on whether or not you speak the language? What other factors influence what you choose to do on this first free day in your metaphorical new home?

Imagine that you've just started a new job or are attending a new school, or that you've just committed to a new relationship or are newly single. What do you do? How do you relate to being in the midst of the new and unfamiliar?

Many of us respond to the unfamiliar by trying to transform it into something familiar. We want to make sense out of non-sense. We want to understand the reasons, causes, advisability, and risks of unfamiliar behaviors or unexpected outcomes. When we're living or working with people different from ourselves, we want to understand why they do what they do. We want to know that their non-sense at least makes sense to them, even if it still seems crazy to us.

Remember Sheila's chicken porridge story? Well, the prelude to it illustrates what we're talking about now.

INDONESIAN BUFFET

by Sheila

When I went to the hotel dining room for breakfast our first morning in Indonesia, there was a nice, big buffet laid out. To our disappointment, however, it was all western-style breakfast foods. We had started looking through the menu to see what the Indonesian options might be, when I noticed a smaller buffet set up in a far corner of the dining room. Menu in hand, I went over to look and—hurrah!—it was all Indonesian food. I asked a waiter if I could eat from that buffet, and he said no. I was surprised and asked again in a different way. Again, he said no. So I ordered chicken porridge from the menu and then, for the rest of that breakfast and for almost all the breakfasts that followed, I tried to figure out why we weren't allowed to eat from the Indonesian buffet. What could their reasoning possibly be? Was it for Indonesians only? Was it for longer-term hotel guests only? Was it only for people eating earlier or eating later? I really wanted to understand! If I could at least know what the reasoning was, maybe I could accept being refused access a bit more easily.

How about you? Do you want to know why Sheila wasn't allowed to eat from the Indonesian buffet? Would you feel somehow cheated if we didn't tell you the end to this story? Or would you assume that we just hadn't written the story very well, that there was an oversight on the part of the authors and the editor and perhaps we'll do a better job when we update the book for the next edition? Is it easier not to know the answer if you think we don't know it either? Does it make it worse to know that, on our last morning in town, we discovered the rule and we're still not going to tell you?

It's interesting, isn't it, how quickly we can feel incomplete even when the information we're missing isn't particularly necessary to our well-being.

> *Many of us respond to the unfamiliar by trying to transform it into something familiar.*

Beyond Merely Tolerating Ambiguity

All of us have a need to know. For some of us that need comes sooner, for others later. For all of us, the need to know arrives when we reach the limits of our comfort zone.

A cultural group's probable comfort zone around ambiguity is often revealed in its language. A verbal agreement to meet tomorrow with a Jordanian friend will often be followed by the quiet phrase "Insh'Allah," meaning "If it is God's will." A Filipino friend might follow such an agreement with "Bahala-na," also meaning "God willing, so be it." A Swiss friend, on the other hand, might pull out a calendar to note the appointment.

If disappointed by a turn of events, a Thai friend might say "Mai pen rai," meaning "It's nothing, no worries"; a USAmerican friend might start strategizing ways to ensure a different outcome next time.

In Japanese, a train does not go "from Tokyo to Kyoto" but from Tokyo "in the direction of" Kyoto; while intending that the train go to Kyoto, the linguistic construction acknowledges that many things can happen and so, ultimately, no one can say where the train will end up.

Of course, there's nothing wrong with needing to know. Needing to know can be an expression of genuine interest in what motivates others, in the cultural and personal values that drive behavior. Indeed, it's important to understand why and how the world makes sense to someone different from ourselves. It's a good thing to appreciate the values that others hold dear, even or especially when they are not our own values. When the need to make sense out of non-sense is rooted in a desire to live productively and respectfully among unfamiliar others, it is a natural part of adapting.

It's different, however, when the need to know is rooted in fear and a desire to avoid uncertainty and confusion. Then, we're operating on the unrealistic assumption that we can avoid uncertainty and confusion. In a complex, globalized world, in a time when the speed of change is continuously increasing, such an assumption is not only unrealistic, it's delusional.

As a response to this delusion, it is very common to hear people assert the importance of tolerating ambiguity. Right along with "value diversity" and "suspend judgment," "tolerate ambiguity" is the new conventional wisdom. As we have already suggested, however, it's one thing to talk about valuing diversity but quite another to actually do so when our deepest values and beliefs are pushed. It's all good and well to talk about suspending judgment, but what does that actually mean, and does it take us far enough?

In his book, *Learning as a Way of Being*, leadership consultant Peter Vaill says we live in a world of "permanent whitewater." In such circumstances, tolerating ambiguity is barely a first step.

Tolerating ambiguity implies that we're keeping a psychological distance from the uncertainty we're experiencing. It implies an attitude of putting up with ambiguity because we have to, but only for as long as we have to. It implies that it's not a pleasant experience, best avoided if we can.

When our goal is merely to tolerate ambiguity, we eliminate the potentially powerful learning that is inherent in not knowing what to do.

> *When our goal is merely to tolerate ambiguity,*
> *we eliminate the potentially powerful learning*
> *that is inherent in not knowing what to do.*

Bringing Forth Creativity

The best kind of relationship we can possibly have with ambiguity is the kind that brings forth our creativity. Remember what we wrote about creativity in Chapter 2? Creativity is stimulated when we approach situations and interactions with curiosity and an open mind. As soon as we assert any kind of absolute knowing, we close ourselves to creativity. Absolutes leave little room for new information and insight, no open space for new possibility. Uncertainty, on the other hand, can be counted on to open us up to the quest. Uncertainty drives us to ask questions, to seek new understanding, and ultimately, to discover a creative new beginning.

Susan Jefferies, in her book *Embracing Uncertainty*, suggests a simple yet powerful practice for opening ourselves to the quest. She offers the "I Wonder" exercise in which we are encouraged to add the words *maybe, I wonder, I hope, perhaps*, and other softeners and qualifiers to any statements we make that resound with absolutes. Try it. It's surprising the sense of freedom that's provided by such a simple change in the way we talk about things.

Of course, to open to the quest we have to be willing to turn around and be in relationship with whatever it is that's making us feel uncertain. We have to be willing to dive right into this feeling that we might more typically prefer to avoid.

The story below is a metaphorical example of what we mean by diving in.

HONEYMOON AT SEA

by Stacey

Several years ago, while on our honeymoon, my husband and I went on a day-long sailing trip in the British Virgin Islands. Not long after we set sail into rough early morning waters, I started to get nauseous. Really nauseous. The boat and my body lurched about as we went up one side of an ocean wave and then dropped abruptly down the other side into the bottom of the swell.

I had always heard that the best way to fight motion sickness is to look at an unmoving point on the horizon, so I did that. I tried very hard to disconnect myself from the ocean, to imagine myself out there on that unmoving and stable horizon. To my great embarrassment, however, I spent most of the two-hour journey to our first island stop hanging over the back of the boat. (You can fill in the obvious details.) My husband eventually joined me there, making for some unique honeymoon bonding.

As we approached our first anchor, we were desperate get to the solid ground of the white-sand beach. We said as much to one of the crew members and were surprised by her response. She recommended that instead of running for shore we jump in the water: "The best way to re-equalize your body is to move *with* the sea, not to run away from it." I was skeptical, but I was also feeling so horrible that I was willing to try almost anything. And so, as soon as we anchored, my husband and I jumped in the water. Immediately, the nausea vanished and my sense of equilibrium was restored.

Assuaging our insecurity and doubt with more and more precise planning does about as much good as yearning for the white-sand beach when we're seasick. Next time you find yourself responding to uncertainty by trying to get all the answers clearly defined, see what happens if you release for just a moment from the need to know. See what happens if, instead, like Sheila in the next example, you can hold an openness of heart and mind. More often than not, good things come out of holding open to the possibility of new outcomes.

GETTING A VISA

by Sheila

I was living and working in Japan but didn't have the proper long-term visa. After just three months of teaching, I did what everybody does: I went to Korea for the weekend to get a new visa. The Seoul visa office was quick and efficient; I was in and out in 40 minutes. Now I had time to see the city! I had a good visit and returned to the airport to check in at the Korean Air Lines (KAL) counter for my flight back to Tokyo. Oops! The visa office had not been as efficient as I had thought. My new visa was stamped with the year 1986 instead of 1996. "Please come this way," said the KAL attendant, and there I was, with no passport, sitting all alone in an empty hallway, just watching the clock on the wall as my departure time got closer and closer.

Just sitting there, I was aware that I had a lot of choices. I could get really nervous and angry. I could think about the worst-case scenario, for I had three classes and a faculty meeting the next day and what if...! I could get up and start going into the mostly empty offices looking for someone to find out what in the world was going on and to make sure the officials knew this was not my fault. I could blame myself for not remembering to check the visa before leaving the office; after all, I know that bureaucratic mistakes easily happen. Or I could just give up and take on a "well, I don't really care what happens" attitude. It really was all up to me.

I decided to sit quietly where the KAL agent had left me, focus on my breath, and be as present as I could possibly be to all of the uncertainty. One thing I knew was that anxiety would not help at all. Sitting there was extremely intense. I felt like I was sitting in a fire pit of ambiguity. Sometimes I felt neutral, open to whatever happened, and sometimes I slipped into fear, anger, and self-blame. Each time I slipped, I was able to keep coming back to neutral. I also felt very alive and active even though I wasn't running around trying to find out what was going on.

With 15 minutes to go before the plane took off, the KAL agent came back and handed me my passport. I was allowed to board the plane and return to Japan. I remember thanking her and at the same time thinking to myself that there was no way I could make the flight now. Even so, I took off running and got to the plane just before they closed the door. Imagine my surprise when they ushered me to a first-class seat! I smiled all the way back to Tokyo.

This was a serious situation for Sheila, with potentially serious consequences. If she had missed the plane, she would have missed three classes and an important meeting. She made three key choices. First, she chose to recognize that she was in the midst of enormous uncertainty. Second, she chose to take personal responsibility for the internal experience she would have in the midst of that uncertainty. And third, she chose to dive into the experience of uncertainty as a neutral energy, not as a matter of big crisis or drama. She stayed focused on her breathing and used it to bring herself back to a calm and trusting state whenever she started to get anxious. Ending up in a first-class seat was a delightful surprise.

There's ultimately little value in trying to force certainty to come before its time. Barbara learned a valuable lesson about that standing in the shower of a hotel bathroom in Denver.

HEALTH DECISIONS

by Barbara

I had been diagnosed with cancer, had had surgery, and was now having to decide about next steps. I had researched the allopathic approaches being recommended to me and the naturopathic approaches that were potential alternatives, had weighed all the pros and cons and assessed all the possibilities, and still had no idea what to do. I went to Denver for a meditation seminar, setting the intention that at the end of the weekend I would know the next steps to take. Driving back to the hotel after the last session, however, I discovered I was in as much uncertainty as ever. I felt desperate and started to cry. Returning to my hotel room, feeling a bit damp from the tears, I got in the shower. The running water soothed my sobs but I could hear the same question repeating over and over inside me: What am I going to do when I get back home? What am I going to do when I get back home?

Suddenly I realized that I was seeking certainty before its time. I was asking about what I was going to do when I got home, yet right now I was standing dripping wet in a hotel shower in Denver. I didn't need to know what I was going to do once I got home; I didn't need to know until I was *at* home. In fact, I didn't really need to know until I was in the meeting with my oncologist. From one moment to the next, the need to know lifted and I relaxed into not knowing.

The epilogue to this story reinforces the lesson that we may as well relax into ambiguity until the time to know has arrived. Barbara got back home to find a message from her oncologist. She had looked at the original pathology slides rather than relying on the pathology report alone, and had determined that the cancer posed no ongoing threat; there was no need for Barbara to have any kind of allopathic follow-up at all.

> *Uncertainty can be counted on to open us up to*
> *the quest. Uncertainty drives us to ask questions,*
> *to seek new understanding, and, ultimately,*
> *to discover a creative new beginning.*

Legitimize *Not Knowing*

There is a word—*limnos* in Greek, *limnen* in Latin—that translates into English as "liminality." Liminality means threshold. It's the hallway where Sheila waited; it's the shower where Barbara stood. Any time we are in transition and have not yet settled into our new reality, when we are on the threshold between what was and what is to be, we are in liminality.

There's great creative power in naming and claiming liminal space. Doing so asserts that not knowing is just as real and legitimate an experience as knowing. It reminds us that however uncomfortable we may be with the ambiguity, it's the honest description of what is going on. The example that follows shows what can happen when we legitimize ambiguity and claim its presence.

LEADERSHIP STYLES

by Mr. Nagano

As employees in a global corporation, we Japanese and American managers had received training about the cultural differences in our leadership styles. In the classroom, we could intellectually understand these differences.

However, actually using this knowledge in our new manufacturing plant and office was a different story. We were not really in a Japanese company and we were not really in an American company.

For the first three months, it was pretty confusing and frustrating. Our subordinates, from both cultures, complained about what they called a lack of leadership in us. "The Americans do not give guidance and do not care about us." "The Japanese bosses treat us like children and do not respect us." We were working under tight time schedules and quality requirements, and it was very difficult for all of us not to negatively judge one another.

There were some from both cultures, however, who were better able to escape this trap of totally buying into their own usual ways. They were somehow able to avoid making up explanations for things they didn't understand; instead, they asked questions as though they really did not know what was going on. They got to be better and better observers and listeners. They learned from each situation how to work more effectively with both bosses and subordinates, and they talked about that. Their behavior became infectious, and over the year of the project, many of us began to have good conversations about what was going on.

But, for others, thinking that they knew how good bosses and subordinates *should* behave was a major barrier.

Within the overall ambiguous environment of a not-quite Japanese and not-quite American manufacturing plant, a few key managers escaped the trap of their own cultural certainty; they intentionally created a space of not knowing. Naming and claiming this liminal space allowed them to explore and to learn, to be curious and open. They did this in a highly pressured work environment, recognizing that their communication and leadership difficulties were directly affecting the plant's productivity. From their conversations came new understanding as well as new ideas about how to work together.

When we feel secure that we have *it* or *them* all figured out, we pull in our antennae, explore less, and forget to be curious. We easily miss the important information that falls outside our comfortable and habitual explanations of why something we're doing works or doesn't. As Mr. Nagano concluded, that is a major barrier to success in situations of change and difference.

What might it be like if we never assumed final certainty?

In his book *Only Don't Know,* the Korean Zen master Seung Sahn states that a not-knowing mind is a clear mind. Similarly, Indian philosopher and beloved teacher Jiddu Krishnamurti wrote in *Freedom From the Known,* that what we know imprisons us. Both teachers suggest that certainty is an illusion, one that doesn't serve us well as we navigate a world vast in its diversity. From their perspective, a not-knowing orientation is the path to wisdom.

Eminent western scientists have said much the same, among them two physicists. Richard Feynman is a Nobel laureate for his work in electrodynamics. In *The Meaning of It All,* he emphasizes the importance of freeing ourselves from the known. He interprets this as the freedom to doubt. He writes, "If you know you are not sure, you have a chance to improve the situation. I want to demand this freedom for future generations" (p. 28). Renown quantum physicist and author (most notably of *Wholeness and the Implicate Order,* and *On Dialogue*), David Bohm also emphasized recognizing that our thoughts are merely one form of perception. Incidentally, he and Krishnamurti engaged in deep dialogues about whether and how it is possible to both think and become aware of thoughts at one and the same time.

Personal Leadership practitioners often say that this practice of engaging ambiguity is at first the most difficult one of the six to understand. Almost invariably, however, they also say that it becomes the most freeing.

There's great creative power in
naming and claiming liminal space.

Try This: Learning Through Ambiguity

Step One. Create opportunities to get lost and experience your response to ambiguity.

- Go somewhere you've never been—for example, to a part of town that's unfamiliar or to a class teaching some skill you've barely even heard of. Commit at least 15 or 20 minutes to being there in the midst of the unfamiliar.

- Focus on your responses. What are your standard coping mechanisms? What are your habitual responses to not knowing? Do you have a tendency to want to fill in the space with knowing, with a plan, with causes and reasons? What judgments, emotions, and physical sensations do you experience when you don't know what to do or say or think?

- Towards the end of this time of being lost, reframe what you are doing into a purposeful game, a kind of treasure hunt. What happens as you now allow yourself to be in a process of moment-by-moment discovery, letting each piece you discover lead you into the next?

Step Two. Pay attention to your experience when plans you have—something you were particularly looking forward to—suddenly change.

- As soon as you can, take a moment to identify all your expectations and the outcomes that were supposed to result from your original plans. Now, metaphorically pick them up and set them aside.

- Consider what might be possible if the new circumstances were actually an opportunity being presented to you. Rather than focusing on a problem to be solved, ask yourself what might be possible in the new situation?

- If you feel especially emotional, try taking a walk, exercising, dancing, or painting. That is, do some physical or kinesthetic activity to move your attention from your head more into your body and to help release the emotion about the change of plans. Notice when you feel more calm and balanced.

- As you feel more calm and balanced, begin to focus on your breathing, consciously breathing in and out of your heart area. Begin to ask yourself these questions:
    - "What else is possible that I was not aware of before?"
    - "How is this situation serving me and teaching me, leading me in new directions?"

      – "How can I widen and deepen my awareness of this situation?"

      – "How can I most appropriately respond to this situation?"

Step Three. Relax and reflect.

- What patterns do you see in the way you respond to uncertainty and change? What kind of relationship do you seem to have with ambiguity?
- What happened when you started to relate to the unknown as a treasure hunt? What happened when you started looking for the opportunity presented by the change of plans?

To Summarize

- Engaging ambiguity can be the most difficult of all Personal Leadership practices, but once we begin to get it, it can also be the most freeing.
- It is appropriate to want to understand what drives the behaviors of people who are different from us. However, it is delusional to try to escape the uncertainty and the confusion such differences arouse.
- The not knowing of liminality, of that in-between place, is a very legitimate, creative, and powerful place to be.
- Dive into the ambiguity and remember: you don't need to know until you need to know!

CHAPTER EIGHT

Practice: *Aligning With Vision*

The carv'd riverbed
Winds its way through rugged land
The river flows with all ease.

Visions provide direct support as we live and work in situations of difference. Craft your guiding vision. Commit to being an expression of your highest and best. Make choices that support you living in alignment with your vision.

We come now to the sixth practice of Personal Leadership. People new to the methodology might find this the easiest practice to understand. After all, the idea of writing a personal vision statement has become almost as conventional in its wisdom as writing an organizational mission statement or a project purpose statement. Why, then, don't more of us write vision statements? Why don't more of us use them to help craft the lives we are committed to living? And what is it about vision statements that really makes them useful?

The Power of Vision

It's intriguing to review the breadth of research on the power of vision. Much of it can be traced back to the mid-1950s and the publication by Robert Merton of *Social Theory and Social Structure*. In that book, Merton coined the term "self-fulfilling prophecy." That is essentially the power of vision: what we prophesy, in particular what we put our attention and commitment to, becomes what we bring forth.

What we prophesy becomes what we bring forth.

Medical Research. The "placebo effect" is a phenomenon first identified in the medical arena. It is now relatively well-known by the general public, but is still often treated with skepticism outside the medical community. It describes the profound effect exerted by the mind on our physical well-being. A 2002 Discovery Channel production, *Placebo*, presents key empirical research documenting how a sugar pill disguised as medication can, in particular instances, have as significant a positive effect on a patient's recovery as the medication itself.

Research on postoperative recovery is suggesting that if patients have two positive images in their inner dialogue for every one negative image, their surgery will have a much higher success rate, and postoperative recovery will be both faster and easier. David Cooperrider, co-author of *Appreciative Inquiry* and originator of a process technology by that same name used all over the world, speaks about this research in his chapter "Positive Image, Positive Action." So does Peggy Huddleston in her book, *Prepare For Surgery, Heal Faster*. She too invokes the biochemical importance of the mind-body connection and describes research showing that people using her techniques, which help them engage their surgical experiences from a place of profound relaxation and peace, use up to 50% less pain medication and heal notably more quickly. Workshops in her technique are offered in leading hospitals, including NYU Medical Center in New York, Greenwich Hospital in Connecticut, and Kaiser Santa Clara Medical Center in northern California.

Norman Cousins became famous for using laughter to heal himself from life-threatening illness. He wrote about his experience and the potential broader implications in several books, most notably

Anatomy of an Illness as Perceived by the Patient, and *The Healing Heart.* He considered positive imagery and positive thought as integral to the healing process. His experiences inspired a research-focused task force whose work ultimately led to the development of the Cousins Center for Psychoneuroimmunology at the University of California, Los Angeles.

This kind of medical research on the power of the mind-body connection speaks directly to the power of vision: when we craft a vision with clear detail and hold it with mindful intention, something physically tangible is activated.

Medical research on the power of the mind also suggests that placebo effects are strongest when members of a group, and not just a single individual, share a belief in the effectiveness of the treatment. In other words, a positive vision has even more power when the whole team together constructs and commits to the vision.

> *When we craft a vision with clear detail*
> *and hold it with mindful intention,*
> *something physically tangible is activated.*

Sports Research. Stephen Covey, in *The Seven Habits of Highly Effective People,* says that successful leaders do everything twice, first in the mirror and then out in the world. So too do successful athletes.

Indeed, the power of vision is such that simply visualizing yourself engaging in a particular physical skill helps you build the necessary muscle memory to then perform that skill in reality. This was documented in a frequently quoted research study conducted by Australian psychologist Alan Richardson and discussed in Michael Talbot's book, *The Holographic Universe.* Richardson randomly selected three groups of basketball players and tested them on their ability to make free throws. Over the next 20 days, all three groups followed a specific routine: the first group did not practice at all, the second group spent 20 minutes each day practicing free throws, and the third group spent 20 minutes each day simply imagining themselves making free throws. If anyone in the third group missed a shot in his imagination, he was told to see himself making a successful free throw.

The results are fascinating. The group that didn't practice showed no improvement after their 20 days. The second group, which actually did practice, improved by 24%. The third group, the one whose members practiced only by imagining themselves making successful free throws, improved by 23%.

Michael Gelb, producer of the audio recording *Creative Genius*, offers a similar example on the power of vision. He tells the story of Major James Nesmith whose golf game improved while he was a prisoner of war (POW) in then–North Vietnam. Each day of the seven years Nesmith spent as a POW, he imagined himself playing 18 holes on the golf course near his home. An average golfer with scores in the 90s, he says he kept himself sane while isolated in his small cell by imagining the smell of the grass, the feel of the swing, the sound of the club on the ball, the sight of the ball flying through the air. His visionary golfing was very much a multisensory experience. In fact, he filled in the details of each step along the course so thoroughly, that it took as long to play in his mind as it did to play in actuality. Every day for those seven years of captivity, Nesmith played a perfect game of golf. The first time he played 18 holes of golf after his release, he had improved his game by 20 strokes; he shot a 74.

While it's enticing to think that one can improve as much by sitting and visualizing as by actually doing, what's really striking in these stories is the importance of practicing with one's whole self— with mind and heart as well as body. In his documentation of the basketball experiment, Richardson wrote that the most effective visualization takes place when the person really feels and sees what he is doing. Those visualizing the free throws, for example, concentrated on actually feeling the ball in their hands, hearing it bounce, and seeing it go through the hoop.

Also of critical importance is the focus on visualizing success rather than failure. Nesmith played a *perfect* game of golf each day that he was in his cell; those making free throws were encouraged to see the ball fly effortlessly through the hoop.

In "Positive Image, Positive Action," Cooperrider calls visualizing success the "affirmative function" (p. 45) of visioning. He states it is quite possible that the best athletes are as successful as they are because they are able to systematically observe and analyze successful performances (positive self-monitoring), differentiate those from unsuccessful performances (negative self-monitoring), and choose between the two cognitive processes. Cooperrider notes that research is increasingly documenting that, contrary to the tendency many of us share for negative self-monitoring, positive self-monitoring seems to be much more effective in building skills.

Focus on visualizing success rather than failure.

Educational Research. The power of a positive vision applies not only to how we think of ourselves and our own futures, but also to how we think of other people. The most famous example of this comes from research that documented what is known as the "teacher-expectation" effect or, more commonly, the "Pygmalion" effect. (It is named after the play by George Bernard Shaw that was translated into film as *My Fair Lady*. In the film, Audrey Hepburn's character, Eliza Doolittle, explains that the difference between a lady and a flower girl depends on how she is treated.)

Cooperrider discusses the Pygmalion effect in "Positive Image, Positive Action." In a classic study, teachers are told that, based on credible information, one group of their students has exceptionally high potential and another group does not; the teachers are thereby led to hold a positive image of the first group of students and a negative image of the second. The teachers don't know, however, that the high-potential students have actually been selected at random and that, in objective terms, all the students have the same potential for success.

What happens as the experiment unfolds is very telling, and has been replicated over the last 20 years in literally hundreds of empirical studies. Subtle differences begin to emerge between the students deemed to have high potential and the rest, based not on any innate capability, but only on the directed expectancy held by the teacher. At the end of the year, teachers deem the second group to be much more troublesome than the first. More striking still, by the end of the year the first group is deemed more successful than the second based on objective measures.

Educators had to stop doing research like this because of increasing ethical concerns: they found that the power of expectation was so strong that the objective differences between the two groups of students, generated by the artificially directed expectations of the teachers, continued even over seven years.

The power of a positive vision applies not only to how
we think of ourselves and our own futures,
but also to how we think of other people.

Stepping Up the Stairs

One possible reason more of us don't write vision statements—or personal and professional mission statements—is that we don't know what to do with them once we have them. Vaclav Havel, former president of the Czech Republic, is frequently quoted as saying: "Vision is not enough. It must be combined with venture. It is not enough to stare up the steps, we must step up the stairs."

Our visions can help us step up the stairs by serving as our beacon, as our support, and as our compass. Esther's vision did exactly that for her when she was confronted by a very difficult time.

A FRIEND'S DEATH

by Esther

My friend was suffering from a lung cancer that was advancing very aggressively. We finally got the call we dreaded. He was in his final stages of dying and we were called to come to his side. We flew to be with him immediately. We did not know if we would get there in time to see him alive. As I rushed about getting ready to fly, I remembered my vision—"be a good witness."

A USAmerican of European ancestry, my friend had chosen to make his home in Mexico more than a decade before. Estranged from his birth family who had issues with him being gay, he had a created a very strong community of support. These friends now turned out to help, all of them Mexican and all of them gay. In traveling to Mexico, I knew I was in for a huge experience: a dear friend dying, an unfamiliar health care system in an unfamiliar country, estranged and homophobic siblings, his closest Mexican friends feeling overwhelmed....

As soon as my husband and I arrived, it was clear that the intersecting point between Mexico, our friend's family, and our friend's friends was full of misinterpretation and miscommunication: chaos was occurring. No one was in charge of his medical bills; no one was in charge of his consulting business; no one was in charge of his household. Disagreements arose between the family members and close friends about all of these issues. We were caught up in the chaos of our loved one dying and all the questions about the details of his life. He himself was in a medically induced coma as the team of doctors tried to plan procedures that might prolong his life even just a bit.

As each of the enormous issues and concerns surfaced, I could easily have been swallowed up in the grief and other strong emotions around us. I paused many times a day, for weeks, catching my breath and trying to relax as people screamed at each other—probably in hurt and surprise and cultural confusion as much as in anger.

Each time I took a breath I focused on my vision. The phrase "be a good witness" allowed me to gain a perspective outside of my own emotions, judgments, and sheer exhaustion. Though I was impacted by all that was going on around me, I kept my perspective. Time after time, I was able to find the right thing to do or to say. I remember being amazed as I navigated the many different challenges presented each day, all with an equanimity that at the time seemed uncharacteristic of me.

As a beacon, our vision can inspire us towards our highest and best. As a relief, it can comfort and reassure us in times of difficulty or stress. As a compass, it can give us practical direction for decisions we are making. Our vision can be all of these things to us in turn, and sometimes even all at once.

For our visions to serve us in this way, they must be authentically our own, driven by what we care about most. Tony Loehr and Jim Schwartz report on a study by the University of Rochester, Human

Motivation Research Group, in their book *The Power of Full Engagement*. The study demonstrated that people whose motivation arises from within, based on their own deep values (they call this authentic motivation), exhibit more interest, excitement, and confidence, as well as greater persistence, creativity, and performance, than a control group of subjects who were motivated largely by external demands and rewards.

When our vision is authentic, like Esther's, it provides us with a powerful motivating beacon. It can also serve to quickly reorient us to our Personal Leadership practice, and can give us comfort and reassurance by reminding us that we have the capacity to deal with whatever is facing us. That was the case for Megumi.

RUSH HOUR IN TOKYO

by Megumi

After my quiet and peaceful time in the mountains, I returned to Tokyo last night. When I met the rush hour crowd in Shinagawa station, I was almost defeated by the reality of Tokyo life. But I soon recovered by remembering my vision of being at my "highest and best." What an empowering feeling!

One of the greatest gifts a vision statement offers us is the way it can guide our decisions. A well-crafted and authentic vision statement can serve as a compass for how we want to be in the world, and can help us determine how best to respond to a particular situation or person.

TEACHING GRADE TWO

by Delsey

Ever since the first day of school, Bobby had caught my attention. In my classroom of first and second graders, Bobby stood out—mostly due to his size and his behavior. I observed the classroom carefully and watched the interactions between my mentor teacher and the students. I paid particularly close attention to her style of classroom management. This school uses a "time-out" policy. Students who act out or disrupt the class are asked to go to time-out, which means they leave the room and go to another classroom for some "think time" before returning to their regular room. After the first few weeks of school, Bobby had already established a set pattern of behavior within the classroom and was considered a frequent user of the time-out system.

I disapproved of the way the time-out system was being used with Bobby. I knew that given the chance I would definitely handle his behavior differently than my mentor teacher was doing. I had full confidence that I had the patience and understanding necessary to deal with this child in a more productive manner.

Several weeks later, my mentor teacher was absent and I was given the opportunity to teach the class for the entire day. During the morning session, Bobby was particularly disruptive and had an angry attitude. As the only adult in charge, I noticed that my idealistic patience was quickly wearing thin. The stress of teaching the class and maintaining order with Bobby's outbursts started to frustrate me. I gave him several warnings, and then I finally sent him to time-out—exactly as I had seen my mentor teacher do so many times before. I was devastated. I had done exactly what I had told myself I would not do.

As I walked around helping students with the project they were working on, my mind was swirling with thoughts about Bobby. I kept asking myself, "What about my vision?" The teacher who sent Bobby to time-out looked nothing like the teacher of my vision. I struggled with the discrepancy while I continued to teach.

The time-out system works well for many of the students in our classroom. For the teachers, it is also often the most convenient way to deal with disruptive behavior. It was clear to me, however, that Bobby needed something else to motivate him to make better choices in our classroom. My vision of being an excellent teacher wouldn't allow me to take the convenient route; I had to find what was best for Bobby.

Over the next weeks, I had a heart-to-heart talk with Bobby. He told me that he has a hard time not blurting out in class. I told him that he has great ideas and many positive things to share, but that he needed to remember to raise his hand. I gave him some suggestions on how he could use his words and actions to control his impulsivity. I also decided to ignore his outbursts and disruptions during my teaching time (thus not giving him negative attention) and instead focused on praising the students who were doing the right thing (such as raising their hands to speak). Bobby started to realize that the only way he would get my attention was if he raised his hand.

This has taken a great deal of time, but I am now starting to see the positive effects of this change. Now, instead of asking Bobby to go to time-out, I am able to say, "Thank you for raising your hand, Bobby!" These are small steps, but at least it has given Bobby more opportunities to stay in the classroom—which means more opportunities for him to learn. I would like to think that by changing the way I interacted with Bobby, I am inspiring and empowering him to take responsibility for his own learning, thus giving him the hope, the motivation, and the tools to succeed long after he has passed through my classroom. My actions with Bobby are now directly in line with my vision for teaching.

Thanks to Bobby, I've realized that all of my students are unique individuals who need different things from me to motivate and guide them in their learning process. More specifically, my experience with Bobby has helped me discover that staying true to my vision for teaching is a choice I need to make daily.

Delsey came to recognize what Loehr and Schwartz say in *The Power of Full Engagement*: only when we regularly revisit our vision "can we ensure a strong, continuing connection to the unique source of energy such a statement provides" (p. 176).

For our visions to serve us,
they must be authentically our own,
driven by what we care about most.

Key Qualities for a Powerful Vision

One of the first things people do in a Personal Leadership Foundations seminar is develop their own vision statement. Over the years, and with the insight in particular of Jin Abe, one of our Personal Leadership facilitators, we've developed a very effective way to help participants identify for themselves the key qualities or components they want to include. As they engage in that process, and as they then incorporate those qualities into an actual statement, we ask them to:

• choose an expanded context
• focus on their "highest and best"

- emphasize a "being" orientation
- integrate the four Ps

We'll discuss each of these now in turn.

Choose an Expanded Context. Most of the time when we introduce Personal Leadership to individuals and teams, we're doing so in a professional context. You may yourself be reading this book with a professional focus—perhaps you want to strengthen your capacity to work effectively with colleagues or clients who are culturally different than you, or you want to creatively engage the challenges of a new job in a new country.

However, even if you're exploring Personal Leadership for professional reasons, it's useful to remember that our professional selves exist within a bigger context. Who we are as professionals is contextualized by who we are in our personal lives. In turn, who we are in our personal lives is contextualized by our higher order values and/or any faith or spiritual perspective we may have. Personal Leadership, whether we're engaging it for professional or personal reasons, is ultimately about everything we do, everything we are.

Indeed, this is particularly true because we're talking about Personal Leadership in the context of difference. Increasing our ability to stay connected to learning and creativity in the context of difference is not something we can do during work hours and then leave at the office when we go home. The commitment to practicing Personal Leadership in the context of difference is, necessarily, an every-moment commitment.

So, as you start to consider your vision, choose the context within which you first want to focus. Then, let the context expand; embrace the bigger picture as you let yourself consider the fullness of who you are, of how and where you move through the world, and consider your vision for creatively engaging your experiences in each of those arenas.

Personal Leadership is ultimately about
everything we do, everything we are.

Focus on Your Highest and Best. Personal Leadership is about optimizing our lived experience while confronting the new and unexpected and even the disturbing and unpleasant. That's the fundamental focus—it's not just about navigating life, it's about navigating life absolutely at our highest and best.

So what does this phrase mean, "highest and best"?

KABIR

by Clara

When I first began to conceive my vision, I had to really think about what "highest and best" meant to me. And then I remembered a poem by Kabir in which he says it all so clearly.

He writes about a small ruby that has fallen onto the road. Everyone wants it, but no one can find it. I loved the way he described people looking for it: some went to the east, others to the west; some looked for it in the primitive earth and others in the ocean. But—and this is the part that mattered to me when I was writing my vision—Kabir doesn't go searching outside. He realizes this precious ruby is inside and he "wraps it up carefully in his heart cloth."

Isn't that wonderful? That's my highest and best, that small ruby that is so precious.

Highest and best has to be defined by each of us individually. It's what calls us forward toward the full possibility of who we are as human beings—uniquely me and uniquely you. Even those of us who live primarily in the context of our relationships with others, whose sense of identity is less personal and more familial, are well-served by this process of defining our "uniquely me" highest and best.

It's also important to remember that defining highest and best has to emerge out of a full-body experience. Connect to your mind and think about it: What are the attributes of highest and best? What does it look like out in the world? Connect also to the emotion of it: What emotional tones and nuances do you associate with highest and best? What qualities of inspiration do you feel? And perhaps most importantly, connect to your body and feel it: What's the energetic experience of highest and best? What does it feel like in your heart center, in your gut, in the muscles of your shoulders and back and thighs?

As we define the actual feeling body sensation of highest and best, we find that it's a powerful calibration, a potent way of measuring our internal state. It helps us identify when we're in resistance and when we're in inspiration. It helps us remember to consider which emotional and energetic states most serve us in a given moment. More to the point, it helps us authentically reconnect with our energized self and helps shift us when we're feeling stuck so that we reconnect with what has heart and meaning.

PROFESSIONAL SELF-DOUBT

by Megumi

This morning I woke up feeling "I am not good enough" or "I am not as good as others." I felt intimidated and sad, and was not able to stand tall. I took a deep breath and asked myself "What good does it do to be this way? Does it serve me? Does it serve others?" And I remembered my commitment to hold myself at my highest and best. I know that holding an internal energy state of highest and best serves me and others well, no matter how my efforts in the world compare to others. So I took another breath and came back to my vision. The rest of my day was wonderfully productive.

Sometimes people resist writing a vision of themselves at their highest and best because they consider it grandiose and unreachable. A powerful vision, however, is powerful precisely because of its grandeur. We ask people not so much to set a goal as to make a fundamental choice: a choice, as Robert Fritz writes in *Creating*, "in which you commit yourself to a basic life orientation or a basic state of being" (p. 188). Committing to navigate life at your highest and best is to make a fundamental choice.

The actual feeling body sensation of highest and best is a powerful calibration.

Emphasize a *Being* Orientation. Typically, when people first begin to think about a vision, they think about what they are going to do out in the world. We call these "doing" visions. Personal Leadership, however, emphasizes "being" visions; we emphasize the internal experience of difference much more than we do the external trappings.

To craft a Personal Leadership vision, we don't need to know anything about the qualities of difference that our colleagues and neighbors bring into our lives. If we're in professional or geographic transition, we don't have to know what kind of job we're going to have nor the country or region or culture we're going to be living in. Many of us try to concretize this kind of detail first when we're working on our vision statement, but it is irrelevant in a Personal Leadership context. The doing visions that result tend to be quantifiable: "I will have x number of friendships with people culturally different from myself; I will meet or exceed my company's productivity goals within the first x months of my new assignment."

A being vision on the other hand emphasizes our internal state. What energy experience will we have as we encounter the new and unfamiliar, as we engage the strange and unexpected? Will we feel at ease and relaxed and openhearted? Will we hold ourselves, as Angeles Arrien puts it in *The Four-Fold Way*, open to outcome?

HOUSE HUNTING

by Sheila

I was moving across the country and decided to write a mini-vision about the home I wanted to have. I started to write about how it would have a balcony and windows facing a certain direction, the number of rooms I wanted, what part of town it would be in. As I was writing, I suddenly realized that I was writing the equivalent of a doing vision—it was all about the external trappings rather than the internal experience I wanted to have.

I started to write a more being vision: I would feel alive and expanded in my home. I would feel a sense of spaciousness, with room for everything I love to do in a day, from office to art to working out. I would feel connected to the day and to the outdoors even from inside my home.

The place I bought, one month later, was not anything I could have envisioned in a doing statement. It doesn't, for example, have a separate room for my office and my studio and my working out. I have instead an expansive space with huge windows outside of which are enormous trees and through which I get direct sunlight in the day and moonlight at night. The space is so large that I have distinct arenas for my office and studio, with a gym downstairs in the building for my workouts. It's been a perfect home for me, and I might have missed it altogether if I'd stayed with the external doing vision rather than refocusing on the internal being experience.

As you begin to consider your vision statement, focus on your internal being experience. To the extent that you focus on doing, focus on behaviors that you can enact to support your being state.

> *To the extent that you focus on doing,*
> *focus on behaviors that you can enact*
> *to support your being state.*

Integrate the Four Ps. Finally, when you actually write your vision statement, we encourage you to keep four criteria in mind. Conveniently, the four words describing these criteria each begin with the letter P.

Personal. Your vision statement is about you. It's not about what your colleague or partner or sibling or neighbor does or does not do. It's about you.

Writing in the personal does not mean you deny that other people and systems in the world have an impact on your life. Writing in the personal does not mean that actions and injustices in the world do not affect you. Writing in the personal simply means that you're bringing your power home within yourself and taking responsibility for your own experience.

Positive. Your vision statement is about what you do want to bring forth in your life, not about what you don't. The power of a vision comes in large part from where we put our attention. Put your vision on the positive aspects of what you are about.

Present. Your vision statement is about the here and now; write it in the present tense. When you use conditional phrases like "I will" or "I try," you're always putting off until the future what you really want to commit to right now.

Writing it in the present doesn't necessarily mean that you perfectly embody your vision in every moment. It does mean that you are committed to living it here and now, in this moment—and in this moment and in this moment and in this moment—and not just in some conditional future.

Writing in the conditional reads as if you are someone who generally forgets and only sometimes remembers. Writing in the present tense reads as if you are someone who only sometimes forgets and generally remembers.

When we write vision statements in the present tense, we're asserting that our vision of possibility already exists in its essential core within us. We're saying that we can create it so that it becomes our new current reality.

Passionate. Our vision should express the deepest passions of our true nature. It should give us what USAmericans call goose bumps, what Filipinos and the French call chicken skin.

It doesn't matter if someone else reading our vision statement likes it or not, if it makes them feel engaged or not. What matters is how we feel within ourselves when we read our own vision. Does it resonate with us? Does it speak to and reflect our own truth? Until it does, our vision statement is still in draft form, still in development. And when it no longer resonates, then our vision statement is ready for revision.

Physicist Eric Jantsch once said (as quoted in Cooperrider's "Positive Image, Positive Action," p. 31), "Mental anticipation now pulls the future into the present and reverses the direction of causality."

Add to Jantsch's mental anticipation the anticipation of heart, and what Personal Leadership calls embodied knowing, and there's no stopping the power of intention. It is this power that Personal Leadership is inviting us each to harness and direct when we craft a vision for ourselves.

Here are some sample vision statements offered by Personal Leadership practitioners:

- My contribution of action, intellect, and accomplishment originates in my peaceful and vibrant core. I maintain a learning orientation and engage ambiguity as an ally. I breathe deeply to relax and come back to what I believe. I remember that it's only personal if I choose to take it personally.
- I commit to building good relationships between people and cultures, and to operating at my highest and best. I live with mindful intention. I orient to every experience as a learner, as a creator, and as a cultural bridge person. I commit to joy, connection, and the grace of deep stillness, making choices that call forth my deepest wisdom and potential.
- As an effective leader, I consecrate my time, talent and passion to being a vital presence in the lives of individuals, families and my community at all times, in all places, and with all peoples.

There's no stopping the power of intention.

Try This: Learning Through Vision

Step One. Identify your vision of possibility.
- Think about when you are at your highest and best. What are the qualities and characteristics that you embody? What ways of being and ways of doing do you demonstrate?
- Consider also your role models. What character traits do they demonstrate that might be part of your vision?
- Incorporate very specific images or symbols into your vision; let yourself see it in your mind and heart on a daily basis and let yourself experience the physical sensations associated with it.

Step Two. Engage your vision of possibility.
- Spend time each day, each week, with your vision statement. Read it out loud to yourself. Read it slowly and attentively so that you really hear what you are saying, what you mean.

- Get some craft materials such as clay, decals and stickers, or colorful pipe cleaners and feathers. See what happens if you create a three-dimensional physical representation of your vision. Dialogue with your vision as you make the representative form. What more do you learn about yourself at your highest and best? Keep the form somewhere central—on your desk, in the kitchen—as a totem to remind you about who you are.
- Instead of, or in addition to, crafting a physical representation, paint or draw or dance or sing your vision.
- Become a "what is" person rather than a "what isn't" person. Use your energy and attention to attract what you really want, rather than to avoid what you don't.
- When you find yourself in a challenging situation, visit your vision. Allow this visionary commitment to yourself to guide you, to help you discern the right action to take.

Step Three. Relax and reflect.
- Look for the ways in which you and your circumstances are changing in your preferred direction: we get more of what we pay attention to and more of what we measure.
- When your vision no longer feels alive to you—and visions do change—invite the next iteration of it to come forth. What has purpose, power, and meaning for you now?

To Summarize

- Write yourself a powerful vision about what it means to operate in the world at your highest and best.
- When you write your vision, choose your context and make sure you write it so that it's personal, positive, present, and passionate.
- The power in a vision comes from choosing to live in alignment with it. Use your vision as a beacon, a support, and a compass.
- Live your vision in everything you do!

Part Three

PUTTING IT ALL

TOGETHER

As you start to practice Personal Leadership, you'll discover that while each practice stands alone, autonomous, each is also intimately related to the others. The six practices, in application, are very much interdependent.

Perhaps you've noticed both of these dimensions already: although we introduced each practice individually, we often ended up referring to the practices in relationship to one another. That's because each practice serves to augment and reinforce the others.

Indeed, as individual practices, they are very simple. Put into application as an integrated set, however, they facilitate a profoundly powerful path through times of uncertainty and relationships of difference.

We provide an overview of this pathway, what we call the Personal Leadership Integrative Process, in the first chapter in this section, Chapter 9. In Chapter 10, we then present the process technology that sits at the center of the Integrative Process. We call it the Critical Moment Dialogue (CMD). In Chapter 11, we offer some closing thoughts.

At the end of the book, you'll find additional material designed to help you deepen your understanding of Personal Leadership. First we offer a bibliography of recommended reading, which includes all the references we've mentioned throughout the book. Immediately following that, we've provided a list of websites that may be of interest to Personal Leadership practitioners; here again we include URLs to the websites of all the organizations we mention in the book. We've then inserted five additional examples of the CMD being used in real situations of change and difference. At the very end of the book is information about how to find a Personal Leadership seminar and/or how to join the Personal Leadership Seminars community of practice.

CHAPTER NINE

The Integrative Process

Hen lets pippin fight
Pecking shell she becomes strong
And meets all with ease.

As we said early in the book, many of us enjoy having friends, partners, colleagues, and neighbors who are culturally different from us. We deliberately seek out the new and different, whether in our work, in the places we vacation, in the perspectives we seek to understand. It's nevertheless probably safe to say that even those of us who seek out difference are sometimes "pushed" by the reality of it. At these moments, our habitual patterns and ways of reacting rear up so that we find ourselves enmeshed in judgment, in emotion, in the physical sensation of resistance, all perhaps before we are even aware that some circumstance or interaction has challenged us.

Inspirational situations too can sweep us into enmeshing judgments, emotions, and physical sensations. Remember that Personal Leadership isn't just about disentangling from resistance; it's about disentangling from any and all of our automatic habits. While we may be more able to access our intelligence and creativity when we're pushed by inspiration than when we're pushed by resistance, the point is that we're only going to be at our most competent and creative when we're able to free ourselves from anything automatic and be mindfully present.

This feeling of being pushed, then, whether by people or situations, can have the qualities of resistance or inspiration. Either way, Personal Leadership calls this feeling of being pushed a "Something's Up" moment. Recognizing something's up is the first step of Personal Leadership's three-step Integrative Process model:

1. Recognize Something's Up. Be mindful. Catch and attend to the sensation, the emotion, the judgment. Don't let it slip past you.

2. Invite Reflection. Take leadership of your own experience. Make a choice to explore what your Something's Up has to teach you about your patterns and habitual responses. Engage the Critical Moment Dialogue (a process technology we'll present in the next chapter) and use the six practices of Personal Leadership to disentangle from your automatic-pilot reaction. Achieve a new quality of understanding and inspiration.

3. Discern Right Action. Receive your truth for this moment. What, if anything, do you need to do or say? To whom, when, how?

Personal Leadership Process Model

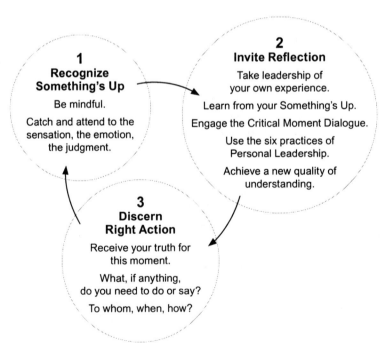

Step 1: Recognize Something's Up

Whispers. Flicker
In the corner of the eye
Fleeting sense – wake up!

The first step in the Integrative Process is very simple. We simply recognize that something's up. We recognize that we are feeling pushed, challenged, and that we are going into resistance (or perhaps inspiration). We may notice that our body has contracted and tightened (or perhaps relaxed and expanded), that emotion suddenly surfaces, that a judgment, positive or negative, about a person or a situation has started running like an endless loop in our brains.

These kinds of sensory experiences ask us to pay attention: something is going on. The more intense the judgment, the emotion, the physical reaction, the more significant the Something's Up is for us; this is true even if, on the face of it, the situation itself is relatively innocuous.

AT THE KITCHEN SINK

by Jeff

I was in the kitchen with a colleague, both of us washing our hands as we talked. I noticed that he left the water running while he dried his hands, and I immediately thought: what a waste! As he continued pressing the point he was making in our discussion, with the water running all the while, I began to get more and more uncomfortable. I wanted to reach over and turn the water off, I wanted to tell him to stop being so wasteful, that clean water is an endangered resource. I found myself getting angry at his careless disregard for our water supply.

On the surface of it, this situation in which Jeff found himself was relatively unimportant. His reaction, however, was deep and immediate. Clearly, something was up!

Do you notice the quality of righteousness in Jeff's experience? The sense that what we are experiencing is the inevitable experience of any sane, intelligent, good person—that sense of righteousness—

is a sure indication that we are having a Something's Up moment. Personal Leadership invites us to be mindful about this, and to take a learning orientation towards it.

Here's another example of a Something's Up moment, this time one that emerges out of an experience of inspiration.

A Perfect Client

by Barbara

I was in a meeting with a client, talking about the design and sequencing of the work we would be doing together. The conversation branched out into how we were going to integrate several core theories and models through the scope of work, and I started to get very excited. I value richly intellectual and abstract discussions that have profound and positive real-world application, and I was in my element. On top of that, I really like the client representatives who were there. I could feel what I think of as the "champagne bubbles" swirling around inside me, the sense of expansive possibility, my whole body leaning forward as I got more and more swept up by my excitement, by my desire to be a part of this project.

Even though we can label the experience Barbara was having as positive, her reaction was as deep, immediate and all-encompassing as Jeff's. That means there's something there for Barbara to understand, something there worthy of a learning orientation. Instead of brushing it aside, saying, "Hey, this is wonderful" or "No big deal," instead of reacting in whatever habitual ways we have in the past, we take a breath for a moment and pause. We recognize there is something here that we can learn from. It may be most especially about ourselves, but is also about how best to interact in this particular moment in the context of this particular situation. That recognition of the Something's Up leads us into the next step: Invite Reflection.

The more intense the judgment, the emotion,
the physical reaction, the more significant the
Something's Up is for us.

Step 2: Invite Reflection

> Open the sewer
> Spread its contents before you
> Only then – lush growth.

Now we come to the heart of the Integrative Process. Although we need to recognize that something's up or we'd never arrive at inviting reflection, it is now that our real attention is demanded. This is where we dig in and sort it out.

We reflect upon our reaction and what it has to say about our habits and patterns. We ask ourselves such questions as: What is going on? Why did I have such a reaction? What am I being shown here about my usual expectations, assumptions, and beliefs? What are the roots, inside me, of this judgment, this emotion, or these physical sensations?

We also reflect on what we know about the other people involved and about the situation. Even more importantly, we reflect on all we may not know.

An important aspect of this phase is to stay in inquiry. It's tempting to look immediately for what to do. If we're exploring a negative Something's Up, we tend to want to resolve whatever discomfort we may have as quickly as possible and get on with life. If we're exploring a positive Something's Up, we may think that we already understand everything there is to know. In either instance, we benefit from staying in inquiry longer than we might usually choose to.

As with any experience of culture shock—and a Something's Up is certainly analogous to culture shock—the best way to resolve our discomfort is to turn around and face whatever we are tempted to run from. The more we turn and face our discomfort, the more we are choosing to be mindful. The more we choose to be mindful and so come to understand our reaction, the more we are able to disengage from it. The more we are able to disengage, the more we are able to access our creative space. The more we can access our creative space, the more we will be able to discern for ourselves the essential truth about a particular situation or experience and, based on that, what our own best right action may be.

The temptation to gloss over the reflective process is perhaps even more challenging when we're exploring a positive Something's Up. We're not then stressed by things going wrong, there's no obvious problem to fix; we just want to go ahead and enjoy the experience.

Jeff and Barbara, to continue with our two examples, could invite reflection of their respective Something's Up moments in many ways. Personal Leadership offers a process we call the Critical Moment Dialogue (CMD). It uses the six practices of Personal Leadership and particular questions connected with each, to facilitate an internal dialogue. As we have said, we will introduce you to the CMD in the next chapter.

An important aspect of this phase is to stay in inquiry.

Step 3: Discern Right Action

The Light shone through him
Her frightening shadow gone
She again saw Truth.

The final step in the Integrative Process is to determine what we need to do. Now that we've mined our experience for the truth it has to give us, the question becomes what, if anything, is the right thing for us to do, to say, to whom, when, and how?

Should Jeff lean over and turn off the water? Should he ask his colleague to do so? Should he let the water run until his colleague turns it off in his own time? Should he chastise his colleague? Should he give his colleague information about the precious nature of clean water, the privilege and responsibility of having access to such a resource? Should he look for other ways in which his colleague is wasteful, perhaps more directly so with funds allocated in the project budget?

Should Barbara continue to express her enthusiasm or rein it in? Should she apologize for it as unprofessional or encourage others to be carried by it? Should she drop the client because she's clearly too invested? Should she submit an employment application to join the client organization? Should she celebrate this client as a manifestation of her perfect customer, and trust that her business will continue to be filled with such high quality opportunities to do the work she loves?

A key dimension to discerning right action is that there is no "should." That is, there is no one-size-fits-all response to discerning the appropriate action for any given moment. Our discernment arises out of the creative spaciousness we have cultivated within by reflecting upon and disentangling from our automatic reaction.

It's important to know that we may end up doing or saying, or not doing or saying, exactly as we would have done had we ignored our Something's Up and gone right ahead with our habitual reaction. However, having taken a learning orientation and invited reflection, having untangled from habit, we can now be sure that we're responding to the new and unfamiliar situation with as much grace and skill, and as appropriately, as possible.

And of course, whatever our response, we then again mindfully notice any Something's Up that may arise in consequence, again take a learning orientation and invite reflection, and again discern our most appropriate and creative action.

So how do we know when we've discerned our right action? It comes through practice, through an increasing sophistication in discerning the quality of our embodied knowing, that is, the quality of energetic experience in our bodies. Certainly, it helps to have an intellectual appreciation for why a particular action seems to be the right one, but we are best guided by a deeper level of knowing: Are we feeling energized and inspired as we contemplate the potential action or non-action? Is there a sense of expansion rather than contraction? The more we learn to distinguish the nuanced messages from our physical bodies, the more we will be able to go forward in confidence with our right action.

"Right" action thus conveys no sense of ultimate truth, but rather a sense of wholeness and completion, of matters clearly perceived and well-considered. In the practice of Personal Leadership, mindfulness and creativity supersede any claim that a right action for one moment is necessarily a right action for any other. To be right, the action must be driven by our full presence, and the creativity we cultivate in any particular instance as we mindfully reflect upon and disengage from our habitual reactions.

Ultimately, what we're looking for through this Integrative Process is what Eugene Gendlin, in his groundbreaking book *Focusing*, called the "felt sense body shift." We call it the "Personal Leadership (or PL) Shift." The PL Shift is the shift from entanglement into disentanglement, from attachment into witness, from righteousness into curiosity and flexibility. The PL Shift is notable: you'll know it when you have it, whether you start in resistance (like Jeff) or in inspiration (like Barbara). The new sense of clarity and direction is palpable, and joyous.

So how long does all this take, from the start of the Integrative Process through to this new sense of joy? It depends. It depends on our skill in practice, on the extent of our entanglement and identification, and on how momentous the situation or interaction feels to us. We can easily move through these three steps as a kind of unified process in just a matter of minutes or even seconds. When the entanglement is great, disentangling can evolve over days, weeks, or even months.

> *"Right" action conveys no sense of ultimate truth, but rather a sense of wholeness and completion, of matters clearly perceived and well-considered.*

To Summarize

- The three steps in Personal Leadership's Integrative Process are:
    1. Recognize Something's Up.
    2. Invite Reflection.
    3. Discern Right Action.
- The process helps us free ourselves from our automatic-pilot reactions whenever we feel pushed, whether that push is a negative or positive experience.

- The process is distinguished by the PL Shift, a very physical experience indicating resolution, to which we can learn to become attuned.
- The purpose of the process is to help us take leadership of our personal experience, and so to help us engage our lives with increasing levels of applied competence.

CHAPTER TEN

The Critical Moment Dialogue

The dog in the field
Loves the grass shaped by turning
Around his center.

The Critical Moment Dialogue (CMD) is Personal Leadership's core process technology for inviting reflection. It uses inquiry to help us apply the six practices to whatever it is we're exploring, and offers a few questions associated with each practice as a starting point for our reflection. The more we use the CMD, the more it supports us in staying in alignment with our highest and best.

We call this process technology a *Critical Moment* Dialogue because we use it at a moment of choice, a moment when we're choosing to discern the essential truth of a particular Something's Up experience. Whether or not the moment is critical to anyone else doesn't really matter. It's critical to us—we are choosing to disconnect from our automatic response and to discern our right action.

And we call this a *Dialogue* because the CMD is first and foremost a dialogue with our own deep wisdom and with the creativity inherent in the situation we're exploring. In this context, dialogue does not mean any kind of conversation or discussion with anyone else. While we may use a CMD coach or partner, as we'll discuss below, a CMD is primarily an internal dialogue.

The Something's Up that we explore as a critical moment may be a positive (happy, inspiring) or negative (difficult, unpleasant) situation. Although we may think more often of using the CMD on a negative situation, the process is equally valuable to use on a positive one. Indeed, the CMD will help us take an appreciative, learning, and receptive orientation to whatever kind of situation or experience we find ourselves in. It will help us step forward with mindfulness, access our creative wisdom, and align with our vision of ourselves at our highest and best.

Whether or not the moment is critical to anyone else doesn't really matter. It's critical to us—we are choosing to disconnect from our automatic response and to discern our right action.

Some Suggestions for Using the CMD

1. *Begin by engaging a receptive orientation.* Find a quiet spot and ensure that you have at least 30 minutes of time for your personal reflection and writing. Begin by cultivating stillness, taking deep breaths, and relaxing. Bring your attention into your heart area; breathe in and out as if from your heart until you feel as calm and receptive as you can be in the moment. When you're ready, begin.

2. *Pay attention to the physical sensations in your body.* As you pose each question and as answers come forth, notice whether you're feeling diminished, heavy, and confused, or energized, light, and alive. Allow the pathway of your embodied experience to guide you as you sense the difference between merely repeating what you already know and gaining insight, energizing clarity, and new perspective. Discover how the critical moment is serving you.

3. *Separate inquiry from decision making.* It is very important to separate your work on the internal dialogue of the full CMD from the ultimate step of discerning your right action. If you don't do this, the process of the CMD can be short-circuited and potential value lost.

4. *Fully engage all perspectives.* When you are engaging in your inner dialogue, you need to be sure to let all your opinions and voices be present. You mustn't be swept away by the loudest voice, the quietest, the most logical, the most emotional. And don't worry if you find yourself writing something rather ugly or mean, especially in response to a challenging or negative Something's Up. The CMD will serve you best when you are fully honest with yourself.

5. *Welcome, and trust, surprises.* You need to be willing to fully welcome surprises and insights that you never could have imagined. In truth, it may be that the more unusual and unexpected the insight, the more you can trust that it is not a replay of the habitually programmed automatic script you have spent years perfecting. You must be mindful of each insight as it surfaces, however small and easily dismissed it may seem at first.

6. *Use vision as a guide.* Remember that the CMD is set within the context of your guiding vision. Your vision is the beacon that keeps you focused when the tendency to diverge or to be less than honest with yourself is strong. Of course, your vision is dynamic and may well be refined through the CMD process. You will be able to tell when it is appropriate to align with your existing vision and when it is time to change your vision.

7. *Make the CMD work.* It's important to remember that the CMD questions are offerings, not strictures. As the practice of this internal dialogue becomes more familiar, questions sometimes seem to collapse in both time and sequence. You may find that some of the questions in the CMD become your favorites because they seem to consistently open doors to new or surprising information. You may also find that you develop new questions that work particularly well for you with one or more of the Personal Leadership practices.

The CMD Questions

Now let us turn to the CMD itself. We begin by summarizing the critical moment: What are the circumstances? What happened? This is where we describe the situation with as little interpretation or evaluation as possible.

We then respond to a series of questions, three allocated to each practice. We don't have to go through the questions in any particular order (nor, indeed, the practices in any particular order), but, especially in the early days of our practice, it's important to answer all the questions under all the practices.

Attending to Judgment
- What is the positive or negative judgment I am having about myself, or about the other person or situation I am facing?
- What positive or negative assumptions am I making about myself, the other person, or the situation I am facing?
- What was I expecting? What is motivating me in this situation? What do I think is motivating the other people involved?

Attending to Emotion
- What are the positive or negative emotions I am having in this situation? What are the qualities and characteristics of my emotions?
- What information are the emotions offering me?
- Why do I care about this critical moment situation so much? Which of my values are involved?

Attending to Physical Sensation
- What is the physical sensation I'm experiencing in this critical moment situation? Where is the sensation located in my body?
- What is the sensation about? What is it communicating to me?
- What do I need to do to feel physically at ease and balanced again?

Cultivating Stillness
- What additional questions, focusing on any of the practices, do I need to ask myself?
- Taking a breath, what insight comes from the silence within?
- What can I learn about myself from this critical moment situation?

Engaging Ambiguity
- What do I not know?
- What more can I not know?
- What can I do to become more comfortable with the ambiguity and/or to get some clarification?

Aligning With Vision
- Where are the gaps between my current reality and my vision of myself at my highest and best?
- How does this situation confirm my vision? What aspects of my vision does it confirm?
- How, if at all, does this critical moment experience suggest I change or refine my vision?

And then... Discerning Right Action
- What might I do to bring my current reality into alignment with my vision?
- What action might best move me towards my highest hopes and enhance the creative potential of this interaction, relationship, or situation?
- What, if anything, is the right thing to do? To say? To whom? How?

Once we have answered the questions, we then summarize our insights and new learning. What have we learned about ourselves? What have we learned about the situation or other people involved? What have we learned about what it means to be effective in situations of difference? What have we learned about what it means to align with our highest and best?

To complete, we check in with our body, our physical sensations. What is our current energy state? Are we feeling inspired and energized? If not, there may be something more for us to receive and we return to whichever of the six practices calls to us for another phase of deepening exploration.

When we feel complete, we check in again with our bodies. If we feel any residual tightness or sense of holding, we get up and move our bodies: we stretch and bend and wiggle our hips, we move in whatever ways our bodies want us to move. We release the energy and feel again a light free-flow within ourselves. We do this until we are complete.

An Example

Megumi wrote a CMD that we offer here as an example of how one person used the process to come to new clarity and a discernment of her right action. Look for the moment when she starts to experience the PL Shift.

CHANGE OF PLANS

by Megumi

Briefly summarize your Something's Up critical moment.

What are the circumstances? What happened?
Describe the situation with as little interpretation or evaluation as you possibly can.

Everything seemed to be going well. I was in Atlanta for a project. I was expecting more opportunities ahead. In the following week, I had six appointments set up in Washington, DC ... all of them were stepping-stones to bigger and better possibilities. And I was stopping in Hawaii on the way back to Japan for a snorkeling/spiritual experience workshop. It was not just for personal relaxation but an opportunity to share time with future project partners. Everything seemed to be in sync.

Then I received a phone call from my father informing me that my stepmother was hospitalized and very ill. Hearing my father's shaky voice, I decided to cancel the rest of my itinerary and return to Tokyo. I made the decision to return not because my father asked me, indeed he did not, but because I had a clear sense that it was the right thing to do. Even so, I felt disappointed and resistant. I decided to learn through and with the situation, and to meet it as much as I could from a place of inspiration.

Right away, I could see at least two meanings for me in this situation. First, I felt I was getting a second chance. What was happening with my stepmother was very similar to the time my own mother passed away. Looking back, I did not do it "right" with my mother. This time I wanted to do it right. Second, I saw it was a gift for me to have a different kind of relationship with my father, to whom I had never felt very connected. I headed back to Tokyo determined to see what was right with the picture.

I've now been back just about two weeks, and I've been going to the hospital every day. Despite my intention to stay in inspiration, I have been noticing that I feel out of equilibrium.

I feel as if I have fallen away from the bigger flow of things ... the flow I was on, the flow that was filled with opportunities. I have found myself thinking that none of the good things I thought would happen will now happen ... I have been imagining that the workshop I am presenting with my colleagues next month at an international conference will be canceled, that I will not be accepted into the advanced degree program for which I have applied, etc. I'm feeling pretty miserable.

Attending to Judgment

What is the positive or negative judgment I am having about myself, or about the other person or situation I am facing?

I am having a hard time staying in inspiration, and that is bad.

The change in my travel plans signifies a downward shift of my bigger life flow. "Nothing will happen anymore."

I have to engage in ambiguity ... that means I cannot do anything, make any plans.

My decision to return was the right one.

What positive or negative assumptions am I making about myself, the other person, or the situation I am facing?

I do not have control of the situation.

Everything happens for a reason ... then what is the reason behind this? Must be a negative one.

To care for a sick relative means I have to drop everything else in my life.

This change was negative.

I cannot make commitments of my own, professional or personal.

I should not have fun when my stepmother is dying.

What was I expecting? What is motivating me in this situation? What do I think is motivating the other people involved?

The situation is an emergency, therefore it won't last more than a few days. Then I can resume my life.

I can face this as a living laboratory for my Personal Leadership practice. I should be able to stay in inspiration as long as I practice Personal Leadership.

I was not expecting how I would be energetically affected by sitting in a hospital room with four dying patients.

Attending to Emotion

What are the positive or negative emotions I am having in this situation? What are the qualities and characteristics of my emotions?

Trapped

Unmotivated

Down, depressed

Out of equilibrium

Righteous

What information are the emotions offering me?

I need a PL Shift!

Why do I care about this critical moment situation so much? Which of my values are involved?

I do not want to give up on my own life, even while I do want to be there for my stepmother and my father.

I want to hang onto my long awaited "good fortune."

I value my independence, my freedom to come and go as I please, when I please.

Attending to Physical Sensation

What is the physical sensation I'm experiencing in this critical moment situation? Where is the sensation located in my body?

Tired … cannot stay up after 10 p.m., barely answering minimum e-mails in the morning before leaving for the hospital. Feeling of heaviness in my chest.

What is the sensation about? What is it communicating to me?

I am more tired than I want to admit.

I need to pay attention to my well-being.

What do I need to do to feel physically at ease and balanced again?

Give myself time to recover from jet lag before reading too much into my current physical condition.

Eat and sleep well ... if things do not improve, think of something else.

Cultivating Stillness

What additional questions, focusing on any of the practices, do I need to ask myself?

My assumptions ... Who said I had to give up on *everything* else, or that all that seemed to be happening before the phone call from my father was good, or that the big flow was not there any longer after I got back to Japan ...? It is all in my mind.

Even when it is not someone's illness, you never know what will happen next. I was operating on the assumption that things would happen in the way that I expected. When I stand instead with the assumption that all is uncertain, then I realize how amazing it is that anything does happen. I'm actually really grateful for all the possibilities that exist for me right now.

Physical sensation ... I did not give myself any time to recover from my jet lag. How much of my fatigue is from traveling? How much is indeed from being in the hospital? It is too soon to say, isn't it?

(I can feel the PL Shift starting to happen! I am starting to feel filled with gratitude, a very different kind of physical sensation than the exhaustion I've been feeling.)

Taking a breath, what insight comes from the silence within?

I've been sitting for short meditations every morning and inviting an angel for the day by pulling angel cards. Not much seems to happen with the meditation....

I already have so much, and so much good is going for me.

I am so supported, loved, and cared for by all my friends and colleagues.

My life *is* going on.

What can I learn about myself from this critical moment situation?

I am very blessed and deeply happy indeed.

(I'm feeling more and more energized as I stay with this acknowledgment of how blessed I am.)

Engaging Ambiguity

What do I not know?

I do not know how long this situation will last.

What more can I not know?

What other doors might this situation open for me? Are the doors that come to me through this situation even more important to me than the doors I thought were in my original plans of going to Washington, DC?

(Yes, this is the right track: I feel lighter, like a big weight has been lifted off me. I can contemplate going to the hospital again tomorrow, and it feels easy.)

How is my being here synchronizing with the bigger flow of things I thought I had fallen away from?

How has it been possible to do all that I have been doing … go to all the places I have been, see all the people I've been with … just being able to lead an ordinary life, how has it been possible? Have I ever really appreciated it?

What can I do to get more comfortable with the ambiguity and/or to get some clarification?

Trust that the universe has a way to take care of me … what needs to stay will stay. Letting go of what I thought I had might be a way to simplify my life.

Accept fully and wholeheartedly all the support that has been offered.

Appreciate what I have.

Aligning With Vision

Where are the gaps between my current reality and my vision of myself at my highest and best?

Am I living my vision of "bringing peace to the hearts…"? How can I bring more peace to my father's heart? To my stepmother? To the doctors and nurses who take care of my stepmother? To *myself*?

"Dynamic in-betweenness of autonomy and interdependence" ... how am I living it? If I devote myself more to the caregiving, can I authentically feel comfortable? Is it then dynamic in-betweenness? If I cut myself off from my ordinary profession and personal life, what does it mean?

How am I expressing "my home within" in each interaction?

How does this situation confirm my vision? What aspects of my vision does it confirm?

I am here to bring peace to the hearts of everyone with whom I interact.

How, if at all, does this critical moment experience suggest I change or refine my vision?

My vision is fine. It reminds me of my bigger purpose, how I choose to be.

And then... Discerning Right Action

What might I do to bring my current reality into alignment with my vision?

What action might best move me towards my highest hopes and enhance the creative potential of this interaction, relationship, or situation?

What, if anything, is the right thing to do? To say? To whom? How?

Give myself permission to do other things, i.e. meeting friends, planning some work-related projects.

Acknowledge all the support, love, and encouragements I am receiving ... all the synchronicity that is happening.

Openly acknowledge the gifts I am receiving.

Put up a poster I drew that reminds me of who I am and what I believe in; that I'm still here.

To Summarize

What have I learned about myself? What have I learned about the situation or other people involved?

What have I learned about what it means to be effective in situations of difference?

What have I learned about what it means to align with my highest and best?
What is my current energy state? Am I feeling inspired and energized?

I am deeply grateful for each interaction and all that happens to me. I've learned a new level of appreciation for ordinary events.

I feed energized in my body. It is even easier to breathe. I have a new sense of peace and calm and well-being. I'm ready to face the day with a smile on my face.

In many ways, reading someone else's CMD is a lot like reading someone else's vision. It's a very intimate experience, and an honor. It may also be, just as with the vision, that what reads to someone outside as a rather calm unfolding is in fact for the practitioner a very profound PL Shift. Here in Megumi's CMD, although we may not experience it as profoundly as she, we notice the Shift beginning to happen and then can even feel the new sense of peace and expansion that she has by the end of the process.

Megumi sent along this postscript:

Since this CMD, I have been consistently feeling deep gratitude. I have been able to help my father untangle from his emotions and clarify his communication with my stepmother's doctors. Indeed, we have a very good relationship with her nurses, who have been very kind. I think my father is doing better with my stepmother's siblings with whom she's had some complicated history. I feel I am gaining much respect from my father. I am better able to have my own boundaries. And I am still deeply grateful for ordinary things that happen, even now, three weeks after writing the CMD.

We have several more CMD examples for you in the back of the book. As you read them, see if you can tell where the PL Shift first begins to emerge.

Formats for Using the CMD

The original format for using the CMD is as a dialogue we have with ourselves, on our own. We sit down with the CMD worksheet, as Megumi did (or go for a walk), and respond to each question. We start with whichever practice seems to be our useful entry point, and we skip around however it serves us best. At the same time, we make sure that we address all the questions. And we pay attention throughout to our physical sensation and to the emergence of the PL Shift.

Over the years, we've discovered that it's also possible—and enormously powerful—to do the CMD with a coach, with a partner, even with a team.

When we do the CMD with a coach, or when we are coaching someone else in using the CMD, it's important to be clear about the coaching role. Coaching in the context of the CMD is about holding the space for the person who is doing the work. We help to make it a safe place, a comfortable place, a place where honest and authentic self-reflection can occur. We pay attention to any tendency we may have to go into agreement: "Oh you poor thing, how horrible that must have been"—or disagreement: "That was unlikely to work; you should have tried something different." When we're coaching someone in a CMD, we never give advice. Instead, we take on the much more helpful neutral stance of the witness and "become" the questions we are offering. The questions from the CMD worksheet serve as our starting point, and we intuit whatever additional questions might be useful to ask.

Coaching someone in a CMD doesn't necessarily mean that he or she is responding verbally. Sometimes people prefer to keep the content of their CMD private, yet still would like the presence of a supportive coach. If that's the case, we hold the space, we take on the neutral perspective of the witness, and we ask the questions from the CMD in whatever sequence we are drawn to asking. It's amazing to discover how spot-on we can be with the questions, asking just the right one at the right time, even when the person we're coaching isn't responding out loud. If the person is responding verbally, then it can be helpful to take notes on his or her behalf.

Sometimes two or more of us are confronted by the same Something's Up. Then we do the CMD as a partnership, or as a team. We respond to the questions together, we explore the full territory—

where our experiences intersect and where they are distinct—and when we have our new understanding and our PL Shift, we discern our right action.

When we coach someone in Personal Leadership,
we take on neutral stance of the witness
and "become" the questions we are offering.

An Important Note

You may have noticed in Megumi's CMD that, just as she was beginning to explore her emotional reaction, she wrote "I need a PL Shift!" Please focus on the deeper meaning of what she meant by that. Do not be seduced by the PL Shift itself. The Shift can come as a great relief, yes, especially when we've been working a CMD on some challenging situation or encounter. The shift in physical sensation from resistance to inspiration, from contraction to expansion, does indeed feel good. And it should: enormous creative energy is released, and we have new insight, clarity, and direction.

The purpose of the CMD and of Personal Leadership, however, is not the PL Shift per se. The purpose is to receive our new clarity. The PL Shift is really a by-product, albeit a valuable one. It offers a way to assess whether our new clarity is indeed new, and not merely a habitual response disguised.

This is an important distinction. The PL Shift must be our compass, not our destination.

In Chapter 4, Attending to Emotion, we discussed the particular way Personal Leadership invites us to orient to our emotions. It is worth revisiting those core ideas here, in context of the CMD and our discussion of the PL Shift.

Personal Leadership emphasizes the importance of witnessing our emotions, of being fully present to their range and depth. It asks us to take a learning orientation towards them, rather than to either act them out on the one hand or suppress them on the other. It reminds us that we must be willing to have the emotion become more intense, just as we must be willing to have the emotion transform and dissipate.

When we make the PL Shift our destination, when our goal is that physical release into inspiration, we're (mis)using the CMD with the hope that our emotion will transform and dissipate. We're "managing" our emotion rather than witnessing it, suppressing it rather than being willing to have the emotion blossom and become more intense.

Personal Leadership asks us to find the middle way, neither intellectualizing our emotion nor engaging in its enticing drama. Esther Louie, a senior Personal Leadership facilitator, puts it this way: "My anger is a life force. I don't quell it or boil it; I move with it." When we use the CMD as intended, it helps us do exactly this. We move authentically with our emotional experience, accessing its full depth and range and the information that it offers us.

The PL Shift must be our compass, not our destination.

To Summarize

- The Critical Moment Dialogue is Personal Leadership's core process technology.
- It offers questions connected to each of the six practices. Answering them helps us separate from automatic pilot and discern our right action for the particular situation.
- There are many ways to use the CMD: alone, with a partner or coach, in a team.
- The important thing is to keep our attention on the core purpose of the CMD: receiving new insight, clarity, and direction.

CHAPTER ELEVEN

A Living Practice

Electron spins right
And a world away in me
Another does too.

Although practicing Personal Leadership is a personal process with the focus first and foremost on taking leadership of our own experience, it is at the same time a very social process. We learn through interaction—interaction with our experiences of daily life, and interaction with the Personal Leadership community of practice.

A Community of Practice

We all participate in numerous "communities of practice," whether we have ever thought of them that way or not. The choir in which we sing, the football team on which we play, the professional associations in which we participate, the gardening clubs and book clubs, the friends we meet at the gym or over lunch; all these and so many more are communities of practice. They help us build our skill, competence, and confidence.

So it is with Personal Leadership. Practitioners participate in a virtual community of practice through which we contact one other for coaching support when we're working a challenging CMD. We celebrate insights and new understandings, and we participate in the evolution of the methodology itself. In fact, since the very beginning, there has been an ongoing community-driven refinement of the language and processes of Personal Leadership. Those who can, meet annually at Practitioner Conferences in the United States and Japan.

For more information on how to get involved in Personal Leadership's community of practice, see page 199.

It's through practice that Personal Leadership
comes alive and begins to serve us.

The Living Laboratory

Taking a Foundations seminar, reading this book, these are all fine and well, but Personal Leadership is just another methodology until we start to practice. It's through practice that Personal Leadership comes alive and begins to serve us.

Students, clients, and colleagues sometimes ask if they're practicing Personal Leadership "right." The only answer to that is a question in return: are you practicing? If you're practicing, you're practicing right. There isn't any wrong way to practice except to *not* practice.

In each moment, literally in each, we have a choice about whether or not to practice. We call it the Personal Leadership "choice point."

This is a moment-to-moment choice between being on automatic pilot and opening up to new learning, to inspiration, to the possibility of strengthened relationships with ourselves and with others. In our experience, the more we engage our lives with mindfulness and creativity, the more we experience the world as a vibrant and deeply fulfilling place. It is a tremendously enlivening process. We find that there's always a new vista around the corner, a new understanding or insight to achieve, a new level of applied competence to actualize. We discover that even the most mundane of activities has the potential to be full of wonder.

Personal Leadership Choice Point

In any context, at any time, in the midst
of navigating any interaction, change, or
difference, you have a choice...

**Do what you've
always done...**

Operate on automatic
pilot, from your habitual
cultural perspective.

**Practice Personal
Leadership...**

Respond mindfully
and creatively to
the unique situation.

And there's no shortage of opportunity in which to practice Personal Leadership, in which to exercise this choice. We're all surrounded by difference and the unfamiliar, all the time. We don't have to wait until we're with someone from the other side of the planet whose language we don't speak; we don't have to wait until we're negotiating an important contract. We can practice Personal Leadership in any place at any time. Even, as Gordon has discovered, while driving a car....

ON THE ROAD

by Gordon

One of the best places to practice Personal Leadership has been, for me, when I'm driving.

My Something's Up moments are relatively innocuous but nevertheless frequent—someone is driving much too slowly, someone else doesn't use a turn signal, the traffic light changes at the last moment and makes me stop. My body gets tense, and I say some rather flippant and not very nice things about people I've never met. I am full of judgments and it's rarely about me or the quality of my own driving.

When I remember to be mindful, I take a breath, access a quiet stillness within myself and a less emotional feeling, and think about my vision. What a surprise: it has nothing in it that says I'm the sole judge and jury of other people's driving expertise! It does, however, say things about living in joy and in positive relationship with difference. Typically, this helps me to relax, slow down, and even laugh at myself a bit.

It's worth noting that there have been several times when having a slower driver in front of me has actually prevented me from getting a speeding ticket on the way to work.

In this simple way, I continue to explore the nuances of each practice and continue to discover their unexpected complexity and sophistication.

Practicing Personal Leadership when the stakes are relatively low helps us build our skill level for when the stakes are higher. We all have access to this living laboratory. Wherever we are, whatever we're doing, we can build our competence to engage difference with grace and skill. It's a bit like learning to swim in the shallow end of the pool: we can drown just as easily in an inch of water as in six feet, but the illusion of safety allows us to focus on improving our stroke.

To Summarize: Making a World of Difference

And we need to improve our stroke! The stakes are high in the world today.

There are huge disparities in power and privilege, in access to what is necessary for meeting even the most basic of human needs. Armed conflicts and territorial tensions abound. Fundamentalism of all kinds—religious, economic, environmental, political, social— seems to be on the rise. Change is the only constant, uncertainty is increasingly the norm, difference is the common thread, and the pace is forever accelerating.

How do we find our path forward in the midst of all of this? How do we find the eye in the center of the storm through which we can discern our own right action?

Personal Leadership offers two principles and six practices and the Critical Moment Dialogue. That's it: very simple on the surface, and as profound as you want it to be the deeper you're willing to go. It's not a magic pill, not a panacea. It's a pathway, part of a network of pathways. It's on offer to those of us who want to improve our stroke and, in the ways by which we feel most called, make a world of difference.

RECOMMENDED READING

The references listed below are drawn from the following fields and disciplines:
- education
- intercultural communication
- leadership
- positive psychology
- sciences
- whole-person self-development
- wisdom traditions

Abe, J. (2005). *Using q-sorting cards for crafting a vision.* Unpublished manuscript, Western Michigan University.

Amour, J.A. (2003). *Neurocardiology: Anatomical and functional principles,* HeartMath Research Center, Institute of HeartMath: Boulder, CO.

Arrien, A. (1993). *The four-fold way: Walking the path of the warrior, teacher, healer and visionary.* New York, NY: Harper Collins.

Bennett, M.J. (1993). Towards ethnorelativism: A developmental model of intercultural sensitivity. In R.M. Paige (Ed.), *Education for the intercultural experience.* Yarmouth, ME: Intercultural Press.

Bennett, M.J. (1998). *Basic concepts of intercultural communication: Selected readings.* Yarmouth, ME: Intercultural Press.

Bennett, M.J. & Castiglioni, I. (2004). Embodied ethnocentrism and the feeling of culture: A key to training for intercultural competence. In D. Landis, J.M. Bennett & M.J. Bennett (Eds.), *Handbook of intercultural training.* Thousand Oaks, CA: Sage Publications, pp. 249-265.

Bly, R. (1973). *Kabir: Ecstatic poems.* Boston, MA: HarperCollins.

Bohm, D. (1980). *Wholeness and the implicate order.* London, England: Routledge and Kegan Paul.

Bohm, D. (1986). *On dialogue.* London: Routledge.

Boyatzis, R. & McKee, A. (2005). *Resonant leadership: Renewing yourself and connecting with others through mindfulness, hope and compassion.* Boston, MA: Harvard Business School Press.

Briggs, J. (1989). Transforming the culture through dialogue: An interview with David Bohm. *New Age Journal, September/October.*

Burns, J. M. (2003). *Transforming leadership: A new pursuit of happiness.* New York, NY: Grove/Atlantic Inc.

Childre, D. & Cryer, B. (1999). *From chaos to coherence: Advancing emotional and organizational intelligence through inner quality management.* Oxford, England: Butterworth/Heineman.

Chodron, P. *The shenpa syndrome: Learning to stay.* Retrieved March 13, 2006, from http://shop.store.yahoo.com/soundstruestore/article-w886d.html

Chopra, D. (1990). *Quantum healing: Exploring the frontiers of mind/body medicine.* New York, NY: Bantam Books.

Claxton, G. (1997). *Hare brain and tortoise mind: How intelligence increases when you think less.* Hopewell, NJ: Ecco Press.

Conner, D.R. (1995). *Managing at the speed of change. How resilient managers succeed and prosper where others fail.* New York, NY: Villard Books.

Cooperrider, D.L. (2000). Positive image, positive action: The affirmative basis of organizing. In D.L. Cooperrider et al. *Appreciative Inquiry: Rethinking human organization toward a positive theory of change.* Champaign, IL: Stipes, pp. 29-53.

Cooperrider, D.L., Whitney, D.L. & Stavros, J.M. (2003). *Appreciative inquiry handbook: The first in a series of AI workbooks for leaders of change.* Bedford Heights, OH: Lakeshore Communications.

Cousins, N. (1979). *Anatomy of an illness as perceived by the patient.* New York, NY: W. W. Norton.

Cousins, N. (1983). *The healing heart.* New York, NY: W. W. Norton.

Covey, S.R. (1989). *The seven habits of highly effective people.* New York, NY: Simon and Shuster.

Cryer, B., McCraty, R. & Childre, D. (2003). Pull the plug on stress. *Harvard Business Review, July.*

Davidson, R. et al (2003). Alterations in brain and immune function produced by mindfulness meditation. *Psychosomatic Medicine, 65,* 564-570.

Discovery Channel (Producer). (2002). *Placebo: Mind over medicine* [Motion Picture]. (Available from: Films Media Group, PO Box 2053, Princeton, NJ 08543 USA.

Ekman, P. & Davidson, R. J. (1994). *The nature of emotion: Fundamental questions.* New York, NY: Oxford University Press, Inc.

Ellinor, L. & Gerard, G. (1998). *Dialogue: Rediscover the transforming power of conversation.* New York, NY: John Wiley.

Feynman, R.P. (1998). *The meaning of it all: Thoughts of a citizen scientist.* Reading, MA: Perseus Books.

Frankl, V. (1984). *Man's search for meaning: an introduction to logotherapy* (third ed). New York, NY: Touchstone Books.

Fredrickson, B. (1998). What good are positive emotions? *Review of General Psychology, volume 2, issue 3,* 300-319.

Fredrickson, B. (2003). The value of positive emotions: The emerging science of positive psychology is coming to understand why it's good to feel good. *Sigma Xi: The Scientific Research Society, July/ August,* 6.

Fredrickson, B., Tugado, M.M., Waugh, C.E. & Larkin, G.R. (2003). What good are positive emotions in crises? A prospective study of resilience and emotions following the terrorist attacks on the United States on September 11, 2001. *Journal of Personality and Social Psychology, volume 84, number 2,* 365-376.

Fredrickson, B. & Losada, M. (2005). Positive effect and the complex dynamics of human flourishing. *American Psychologist, volume 60, number 7,* 678-686.

Fritz, R. (1984). *The path of least resistance: Learning to become the creative force in your own life.* New York, NY: Fawcett Columbine Publishing.

Fritz, R. (1991). *Creating.* New York, NY: Fawcett Columbine Publishing.

Fritz, R. (1999). *The path of least resistance for managers: Designing organizations to succeed.* San Francisco, CA: Berrett-Koehler Publishers.

Gardenswartz, L. & Rowe, A. (1998). *Managing diversity: A complete desk reference and planning guide* (revised ed.). New York, NY: McGraw-Hill.

Gelb, M. (1997). *Creative genius: How to sharpen and intensify your mind power*. [Cassette Recording]. New York, NY: Simon & Schuster Audio.

Gendlin, E.T. (1981). *Focusing* (revised ed.). New York, NY: Bantam New Age.

Glantz, M. & Johnson, J. (Eds.) (1999). *Resilience and development: Positive life adaptations*. New York, NY: Kluwer.

Goleman, D. (1995). *Emotional intelligence*. New York, NY: Bantam.

Goleman, D. (1998). What makes a leader? *Harvard Business Review, November/December.*

Goleman, D. (2003, February 4). Finding happiness: Cajole your brain to lean to the left. *N.Y. Times.*

Goleman, D. (2005, November). *Meditation on the move: From monastery to lab to mainstreet*. Presentation at Washington National Cathedral, Washington, DC.

Goleman, D., Boyatzis, R. & McKee, A. (2002). *Primal leadership: Learning to lead with EI*. Boston, MA: Harvard Business School Press.

Gregerson, H. (2000, March). "Achieving the global assignment advantage." Paper presented at the Women on the Move Conference, London, England.

Huddleston, P. (1996). *Prepare for surgery, heal faster: A guide of mind-body techniques*. Cambridge, MA: Angel River Press.

Hyland, M. E. (2002). The intelligent body and its discontents. *Journal of Health Psychology,* 7(1), 21-3.

Jaworsky, J. (1996). *Synchronicity: The inner path of leadership*. San Francisco, CA: Berrett-Koehler Publishers.

Jefferies, S. (2003). *Embracing uncertainty: Breakthrough methods for achieving peace of mind when facing the unknown*. New York, NY: St. Martin's Press.

Johnson, B. (1990). Being "right" is the easy step. In B. Johnson, *Polarity management: Identifying and managing unsolvable problems,* (pp. 43-51). Amherst, MA: HRD Press.

Kabat-Zinn, J. (1994). *Wherever you go, there you are: Mindfulness meditation in everyday life*. New York, NY: Hyperion Books.

Katie, B. (2002). *Loving what is: Four questions that can change your life.*

New York, NY: Three Rivers Press.

Kim, Y.Y. (2001). *Becoming intercultural: An integrated theory of communication and cross-cultural adaptation.* Thousand Oaks, CA: Sage Publications.

Krishnamurti, J. (1969). *Freedom from the known.* New York, NY: Harper & Row Publishers.

Langer, E.J. (1997). *The power of mindful learning.* Reading, MA: Perseus Books.

Lee, M. (1995). The edge: Playing the edge involves exploring the fine-tuning that takes us even deeper into the experience—in yoga and in life. *The Yoga Journal, March/April,* 104-105.

Loehr, T. & Schwartz, J. (2003). *The power of full engagement: Managing energy, not time, is the key to high performance and personal renewal.* New York, NY: The Free Press.

Maturana, H.R. & Varela, F. (1992). *The tree of knowledge: The biology of human understanding.* Boston, MA: Shambhala.

McCraty, R., Atkinson, M., Tomasino, D. & Tiller, W.A. (1998). The electricity of touch: Detection and measurement of cardiac energy exchange between people. In K.H. Pribram, (Ed.), *Brain and values: Is a biological science of values possible?* (pp. 359-379). Mahwah, NJ: Lawrence Erlbaum Associates, Publishers. Retrieved March 13, 2006, from http://www.heartmath.org/research/research-papers/Touch/index.html

McCraty, R., Atkinson, M. & Tomasino, D. (2001). *Science of the heart: Exploring the role of the heart in human performance.* Boulder Creek, CA: HearthMath Research Center.

Merton, R.K. (1957). *Social theory and social structure.* New York, NY: The Free Press.

Moran, V. (1998). *Shelter for the spirit: Create your own haven in a hectic world.* New York, NY: HarperCollins/Perennial.

Nagata, A.L. (2007). Bodymindfulness for skillful communication. *Rikkyo Intercultural Communication Review, (5)* 61-76.

Opdal, P.M. (2001). Curiosity, wonder and education seen as perspective. *Studies in Philosophy and Education, 20,* pp. 331–344.

Palmer, P.J. (1990). *Leading from within: Reflections on spirituality and leadership.* Washington, DC: The Servant Leadership School.

Palmer, P.J. (1997). Seeking new leadership from within. *The Witness, May,* 6.

Palmer, P.J. (1998). *The courage to teach: Exploring the inner landscape of a teacher's life.* San Francisco, CA: Jossey-Bass Publishers.

Palmer, W. (1994). *The intuitive body: Aikido as a clairsentient practice.* Berkeley, CA: North Atlantic Books.

Palus, C.J. & Horth, D.M. (2000). Leading creatively. *Leadership in Action* (a publication of the Center for Creative Leadership and Jossey-Bass, a Wiley company).

Ramsey, S.J. (1997). Intercultural learning: The present and the possibilities. *SIETAR International – Metro Washington Group News, November,* 3.

Rein, G., Atkinson, M. & McCraty, R. (1995). The physiological and psychological effects of compassion and anger. *Journal of Advancement in Medicine, volume 8, number 2,* Human Sciences Press, pp. 87-104.

Richards, M.C. (1986). *Centering in pottery, poetry and the person.* Middletown, CN: Wesleyan University Press.

Rozman, D. (2005). The zone demystified: An interview with Doc Childre, founder of the Institute of HeartMath. Retrieved March 13, 2006, from http://www.pga.com/improve/features/ mentalgame/heartmath_051005.cfm

Sarno, J. (2006). *The divided mind: The epidemic of mind-body disorders.* New York, NY: HarperCollins.

Schaetti, B.F. & Ramsey, S.J. (1999). The expatriate family: Practicing personal leadership. *Mobility: Magazine of the Employee Relocation Council, 20,* 89-94.

Schaetti, B.F., Ramsey, S.J. & Watanabe, G.C. (in press). From intercultural knowledge to intercultural competence: Developing an intercultural practice. In M. A. Moodian (Ed.), *Contemporary leadership and intercultural competence: Understanding and utilizing cultural diversity to build successful organizations.* Thousand Oaks, CA: Sage Publications.

Schaetti, B.F., Watanabe, G.C. & Ramsey, S.J. (2000). *The practice of personal leadership and the SIIC internship program.* Portland, OR: Intercultural Communication Institute.

Schiller, M., Mah Holland, B. & Riley, D. (2001). *Appreciative leaders: In the eye of the beholder.* Chagrin Falls, OH: The Taos Institute.

Seelye, H. & Wasilewski, J. (1996). *Between cultures. Developing self-identity in a world of diversity.* Chicago, IL: NTC Publishing Group.

Senge, P., Scharmer, C.O., Jaworsky, J. & Flowers, B.S. (2004). *Presence: Human purpose and the field of the future.* Cambridge, MA: Society for Organizational Learning, Inc.

Seung Sahn. (1999). *Only don't know: Selected teaching letters of Zen Master Seung.* Boston, MA: Shambhala Publications.

Shapiro, S., Schwartz, G. & Bonner, G. (1998). Effects of mindfulness-based stress reduction on medical and pre-medical students. *Journal of Behavioral Medicine, volume 21, number 6,* pp. 581-599.

Sher, G. (2002). *The intuitive writer: Listening to your own voice.* New York, NY: Penguin Books.

Sternberg, E. (2000). *The balance within: The science connecting health and emotion.* New York, NY: W.H. Freeman Press.

Stone Zander, R. & Zander, B. (2000). *The art of possibility: Transforming professional and personal life.* New York, NY: Penguin Books.

Talbot, M. (1991). *The holographic universe.* New York, NY: HarperCollins.

Taylor, S., et al. (2000). Psychological resources, positive illusions, and health. *American Psychologist, January,* 99-109.

Thich, H. (1991). *Peace is every step: The path of mindfulness in everyday life.* New York, NY: Bantam Books.

Ting-Toomey, S. (1999). *Communicating across cultures.* New York, NY: The Guilford Press.

Utne, C. (2005). Taking charge of intercultural growth. *FGI World: Redefining workplace health.* (Available from Family Guidance International, Worldwide Headquarters Corporate Office, 60 Columbia Way, Suite 900, Markham, ON Canada, L3R 0C9).

Vaill, P.B. (1996). *Learning as a way of being: Strategies for survival in a world of permanent whitewater.* San Francisco, CA: Jossey-Bass Publishers.

West, M.G. (1997). Don't get over it: The importance of honoring the in-between times. *Common Ground, February,* 22 – 25.

Wheatley, M. & Chodron, P. (1999). *It starts with uncertainty: On leading by letting go.* Retrieved March 13, 2006, from http://www.berkana.org/articles/uncertainty.html

Wolinsky, S. (1994). *The tao of chaos: Essence and the enneagram* (Quantum Consciousness, Volume II). Putney, VT: Bramble Books.

Wright, K. (1998). *Breaking the rules: Removing the obstacles to effortless high performance.* Boise, ID: CPM Publishing.

Yoshikawa, M. (1988). Cross-cultural adaptation and perceptual development. In Y.Y. Kim & W. Gudykunst (Eds.), *Cross-cultural adaptation: Current approaches.* Beverly Hills, CA: Sage Publications.

Zajonc, A. (2007). Contemplative and transformative education. *Kosmos: An Integral Approach to Global Awakening, VI*(1), 42-44.

Zimmerman, J.V.C. (1991). Council: Reviving the art of listening. *Utne Reader, March/April.*

WEBSITES OF INTEREST

All URLs listed here were confirmed on July 2, 2007.

Angeles Arrien
www.angelesarrien.com

Association for Comprehensive Energy Psychology
www.energypsych.org

The Berkana Institute
www.berkana.org

Center for Creative Leadership
www.ccl.org

Contemplative Outreach
www.centeringprayer.com

Creative Mindflow
www.creative-mindflow.com

Harvard Negotiation Project Insight Initiative
www.pon.harvard.edu/research/projects/hnii

Innovation Network
www.thinksmart.com

Institute for Research on Unlimited Love
www.unlimitedloveinstitute.org

Institute of HeartMath
www.heartmath.org

International Institute for Transformation
www.iitransform.com

Mind and Life Institute
www.mindandlife.org

National Resilience Resource Center
www.cce.umn.edu/nrrc

Positive Emotion and Psychophysiology Laboratory
www.unc.edu/peplab

Project Resilience
www.projectresilience.com

Psych-k Centre for Accelerated Personal Growth
www.psych-k.com

Shinzen Young: Meditation in Action
www.shinzen.org

Spiral Dynamics Integral
www.spiraldynamics.net

The Taos Institute
www.taosinstitute.org

The Toltec Teachings of Don Miguel Ruiz and Don Jose Ruiz
www.miguelruiz.com

Zapchen Somatics
www.michaelherman.com/zapchen

And as referenced in the text:

Online msn Encarta Dictionary
encarta.msn.com/dictionary

MORE CMD EXAMPLES

Dandelion fluff
Carried on the wind, also
Arrives at its goal.

In Chapter 10, we reproduced a Critical Moment Dialogue (CMD) worksheet filled out by Megumi as an example of how the CMD can help us release from our automatic habits, come to a new quality of understanding, and discern our next right steps. Now we're reproducing five more CMD worksheets. They are:

- Flying the Flag
- Jumping Rope
- The Post Office
- Co-Creating Meaning
- Playing Jazz

We suggest that you do *not* read these five CMDs one right after the other. If you do, you'll probably find that they blend into one another and generally become mush in your awareness and understanding. Instead, we recommend that you put the book down after each one and come back after a period of time to read another. They'll make more sense to you that way, and be more effective in helping you deepen your understanding of the CMD.

Reading these CMDs is a little like eavesdropping on somebody else's internal process. We've edited them a bit so that they read more easily for an outsider, but even so, remember that you're essentially reading someone else's stream-of-consciousness writing: don't worry if what you're reading doesn't altogether make sense or if you don't quite follow why and how the PL Shift emerged.

Ultimately, as with the practices themselves, the way to understand the CMD and what it offers is to use it on your own Something's Up.

FLYING THE FLAG

by Barbara

Briefly summarize your Something's Up critical moment.

What are the circumstances? What happened?
Describe the situation with as little interpretation or evaluation as you possibly can.

My father turned to look at me as if he didn't know the woman sitting next to him. That shocked me so much that all of a sudden I realized I'd been deeply entangled in a Something's Up moment for more than three months.

It began on September 11, 2001, when hijackers used four commercial airplanes to attack the United States. Thousands died, and people literally all over the world joined with the United States in their shock and grief.

I live in the States. Within hours, U.S. flags began to appear everywhere: hanging in the front windows of homes and stores on every street, flying from car radio antennae, on the lapels of people's jackets at a globally oriented conference I attended two weeks later. The news channels were filled with pundits discussing "Why do they hate us so much?" and in what direction the United States should turn to exact punishment.

In December of that year, I went to Texas to visit my father. There were even more flags there than in the relatively liberal/progressive part of the country where I live. We were out driving one day and a woman cut in front of us on the highway—on the back windshield was drawn a U.S. flag and the words "don't mess with America." I said something about it to my father, turning quickly to look at him as I did so. That's when I saw the expression on his face that shocked me back to myself. Apparently, I had been spilling a torrent of rage, and worse, at the woman in the car and at the meaning to me of the message on her rear windshield, just as I now realized I had been doing at the proliferation of flags over the past months.

Attending to Judgment

What is the positive or negative judgment I am having about myself, or about the other person or situation I am facing?

The people of the United States are myopic, ethnocentric, xenophobic.

They believe we have the right to do whatever we want wherever we want just because we're Americans. They pretend it's for noble purposes, but at best, it's driven by ignorance and more typically by greed and arrogance. All the flags flying are demonstrations of exactly this: people are saying "don't mess with America—let's go bomb them back to the Stone Age."

What positive or negative assumptions am I making about myself, the other person, or the situation I am facing?

I'm right! If our government and the people weren't so shallow and selfish and blah blah blah, they'd know it too.

What was I expecting? What is motivating me in this situation? What do I think is motivating the other people involved?

I guess I was expecting exactly this, which is maybe what makes it so sad. I was expecting that someday U.S. foreign policy would bounce back to hurt us here within the country. I was *hoping* that we might respond with temperance and wisdom, with compassion and a commitment to justice rather than retribution, but I guess I wasn't *expecting* that.

Attending to Emotion

What are the positive or negative emotions I am having in this situation? What are the qualities and characteristics of my emotions?

I am furious, fearful, sad. It is overwhelming. I've been raging for three months and not even aware of it.

What information are the emotions offering me?

I'm furious with the United States and the myopia of its citizens, I'm furious with the world community for allowing the injustices that breed violence, I'm furious with the people who fly the flag.

I'm so deeply sad that we've wasted the world's outpouring of sympathy by asking stupid questions like "Why do they hate us?" and by looking for whom and where we can bomb first.

I'm totally frustrated that once again my perspective seems to be in the minority in this country. And I'm scared of what the United States will do now, of how it will retaliate, and what additional violence we'll generate as a result.

Why do I care about this critical moment situation so much? Which of my values are involved?

I hold a U.S. passport and feel a responsibility to help this country live up to its ideals.

My identity is being challenged by the U.S. response. I have such a deep-seated transnational worldview that I just don't understand a nationalistic orientation—and especially not when I experience it as domineering, self-serving, and patronizing. I'm a dual national and have lived in 10 countries on five continents; I have memories of friends and good people all over, including in countries considered enemies of the United States.

I want something more for our world than people who continue to hate and fight.

Attending to Physical Sensation

What is the physical sensation I'm experiencing in this critical moment situation? Where is the sensation located in my body?

Every time I see a U.S. flag flying, I get scared and I feel it in my heart center and between my shoulders. I feel as if I start to hunch over, close down, tighten up. I also become energized with the feelings of anger, but in a fractured and unfocused way.

What is the sensation about? What is it communicating to me?

That I'm being pushed by all of this! That I care. That I still have big conflicting emotion about what it means to be a U.S. citizen, despite all the exploration I've done around issues of national identity.

What do I need to do to feel physically at ease and balanced again?

Take a breath. Each time I see the U.S. flag flying, take a breath. Breathe into my heart center and let it expand. Intentionally open up, literally lighten up.

Cultivating Stillness

What additional questions, focusing on any of the practices, do I need to ask myself?

What is going on here for me? What is the bigger picture I can hold that will allow me to engage all of this with creativity and intelligence?

Taking a breath, what insight comes from the silence within?

I mentioned identity before—perhaps my Ph.D. research on identity development has something to offer me that would be useful here. Let's see: I read recently that the vast majority of Americans don't have a passport, which means they've never traveled outside the United States, or at least not beyond Canada and Mexico. You don't have to travel abroad to see your home country from a more global perspective, but it certainly helps.

And maybe if they've never left the country, they've never really thought about what it means to be an American in the global context. Being "American" is different when you're cheering an athlete at the Olympics than it is when your country is attacked. Maybe people are flying the flag because for the first time they're thinking about themselves as Americans. After all, the flag is a symbol of the United States; maybe they're flying the flag because they're in the midst of nationality identity exploration—and I know what the models of identity development say about immersing in the identity you're exploring and pushing away for a period of time from the others.

I wonder what can happen as I hold myself open to the possibilities.

What can I learn about myself from this critical moment situation?

The practice certainly never ends. I've been teaching this—Personal Leadership, mindfulness and creativity—for years, and yet this was so big for me it caught me totally by surprise. I was so righteous I didn't even know I was having a Something's Up. Maybe righteousness is a good first clue for me that I've got a Something's Up going on.

Engaging Ambiguity

What do I not know?

I don't actually know why people are flying the flag. What that means to them, what they want to communicate to others by flying it everywhere.

Maybe they're flying the flag because they're in the process of exploring their national identity, not because they've resolved their identity to a nationalistic "let's go bomb everyone" perspective. Maybe I can hold the space for people discovering something new as they do their identity work. Maybe we can come out of this time with more Americans understanding the historic role we've played worldwide, good and ill, and ready to take more responsibility for bringing forth a positive future for all.

Maybe people are flying the flag just to show sympathy with those whose loved ones died in the attacks.

What more can I not know?

I don't actually know that I'm right. I mean, I'm pretty confident that I'm right about the basic stuff about "Why do they hate us?", but I don't actually know the long-term outcome of what's happening now.

I don't actually know that President Bush and his neo-conservative administration—and every administration I've known so far, whether Democratic or Republican—are purposefully self-serving and duplicitous. I've heard it said by people who know Bush that he actually believes he's doing right by the country and even by the world.

What else? I don't know why so many have to suffer, why there has to be such inequity on the planet. I don't know what more I can do about it than continue to live my life as fully aligned as I can with what I believe makes a difference.

What can I do to become more comfortable with the ambiguity and/or to get some clarification?

Breathe, open my heart to others. Notice my righteousness and remember that I don't know, that certainty—even in support of justice and progressive politics—is an illusion.

Aligning With Vision

Where are the gaps between my current reality and my vision of myself at my highest and best?

I'm much more aligned now than I was when I started this CMD. The more I can open to the flags flying and to the people flying them with a willingness to hear their truth, even if it's different than mine, the more I'll be walking my vision of myself at my highest and best. I'm about using difference as a bridge that connects, after all!

How does this situation confirm my vision? What aspects of my vision does it confirm?

That I care about a peaceable world, that it does indeed begin with me and with how I respond to situations that push me.

How, if at all, does this critical moment experience suggest I change or refine my vision?

I don't think there's anything to change, per se. The vision is certainly motivating for me, supporting me in the work of this CMD. I would like to have remembered my vision sooner, but so it goes; I remembered when I remembered.

And then... Discerning Right Action

What might I do to bring my current reality into alignment with my vision?

Keep "peeling the onion" of this CMD. There's a lot here for me still to explore and understand.

What action might best move me towards my highest hopes and enhance the creative potential of this interaction, relationship, or situation?

I could ask the men who live across the street why they are flying the flag. We've always enjoyed one another as neighbors; I know they're not evil people. It would be interesting, perhaps as revelatory as when my other neighbor said he didn't think it was appropriate to respond with violence to the September 11th attacks; I wasn't expecting that from him, I must say!

What, if anything, is the right thing to do? To say? To whom? How?

Most of all it's about me continuing to do my work around this.

To Summarize

What have I learned about myself? What have I learned about the situation or other people involved?

What have I learned about what it means to be effective in situations of difference?

What have I learned about what it means to align with my highest and best?

What is my current energy state? Am I feeling inspired and energized?

I know I'm not done with this one, but a big shift has happened. I feel clear, a sense of lightness in my heart center and actually throughout my body. There's still some tightness between my shoulder blades, so I need to stretch. I can look out the window now at a flag and take a breath and stay open to creative possibility.

Afterword

Six months after doing the initial work of this CMD, I was asked to go to Washington, DC, to work with a group of women from Kosovo. They were in the United States as part of a program sponsored by the United States Agency for International Development (USAID). The program was designed to help them strengthen their leadership skills so they can participate in rebuilding civil society in their war-torn country.

Within the first hours of meeting the women, I discovered they had a very different orientation to U.S. foreign policy than I. When they saw the U.S. flag flying, they described feelings of enormous gratitude, relief, and security. They wanted to meet Madeleine Albright, then Secretary of State under President Clinton, specifically to thank her for the military action she had championed. (I too would have liked to meet Secretary Albright, but more particularly to ask about what I saw as inconsistencies in U.S. foreign policy....)

It was very clear to me that had I not done the work on my CMD, the conversations with these women from Kosovo and their very different perspectives would have been really hard for me. As it was, however, I was able to stay present to them and work with them in a way that served their important purpose—and that, indeed, aligned with my own vision of building a peaceable world.

JUMPING ROPE

by Enid

Briefly summarize your Something's Up critical moment.

What are the circumstances? What happened?
Describe the situation with as little interpretation or evaluation as you possibly can.

It was Tuesday morning of the first week we were in Granada. It was still early, about 6:15. I like to exercise to get my day going, so I was jumping rope right outside my host family's house. I left the door open as I usually did.

I still felt very new to Granada. As I jumped, I was very aware of my surroundings. I had not yet learned to recognize who were regulars on the street. Many people would stare at me when I exercised early in the morning.

This day, I noticed that at the far end of my street two men were slowly walking towards me. The men drew closer to where I was jumping. The first man moved by, maintaining a decent distance. The second man did not. He stopped and tried to get my attention with words like "Como estas?" and "Hola." When I did not respond, he stopped just three feet to my left and stared at me.

Attending to Judgment

What is the positive or negative judgment I am having about myself, or about the other person or situation I am facing?

What was the man's problem?! He was so rude, so inconsiderate and offensive, totally invading my space. He wasn't just staring, he was leering at me in a very sexual way.

What positive or negative assumptions am I making about myself, the other person, or the situation I am facing?

What I'm doing, jumping rope, is perfectly fine, perfectly normal. He's the one being inappropriate. I shouldn't have to change what I'm doing just because he's decided to act so offensively.

What was I expecting? What is motivating me in this situation? What do I think is motivating the other people involved?

I expected him to make a few comments, maybe, and then to move on once I did not acknowledge his presence or reciprocate interest. My silence should have been sufficient indication that he needed to move on.

Attending to Emotion

What are the positive or negative emotions I am having in this situation? What are the qualities and characteristics of my emotions?

I felt uncomfortable and uneasy, unnerved and almost panicky.

What information are the emotions offering me?

I don't like feeling uncomfortable! I am a product of American culture: if something is not to my satisfaction, I want it fixed as soon as possible!

Why do I care about this critical moment situation so much? Which of my values are involved?

One of my values is of having privacy and space. I automatically give it to others, and expect them to give it to me too. He was crowding me in a way that felt very threatening.

I also value the right of a woman to be physically expressive without it being sexual. He was turning my jumping rope into something sexual, and that really made me angry.

Attending to Physical Sensation

What is the physical sensation I'm experiencing in this critical moment situation? Where is the sensation located in my body?

I had a tight sensation in my gut.

What is the sensation about? What is it communicating to me?

I didn't feel safe, even though I was right outside my host family's house and the door was open.

What do I need to do to feel physically at ease and balanced again?

My instinct said that I needed to increase the distance between us, maybe just go back in the house.

Cultivating Stillness

What additional questions, focusing on any of the practices, do I need to ask myself?

Was I getting into a power struggle with him? Was I unwilling to go back in the house because that would have been like letting him win?

Taking a breath, what insight comes from the silence within?

I think I just got very stubborn. Even though I didn't feel safe, I also didn't want to back down.

What can I learn about myself from this critical moment situation?

My values can get me into what I think are intense, one-sided situations.

Engaging Ambiguity

What do I not know?

What about the man? What did he think of the situation? Was he drunk? My host family suggested he probably was....

What more can I not know?

I don't know the local customs regarding physical exercise, whistling at girls, or staring at gringas. I know that jumping rope is an unusual thing, even in the United States; maybe I shouldn't have been doing it here, in a public place.

What can I do to become more comfortable with the ambiguity and/or to get some clarification?

I can try to learn something about the local custom, whether it was me somehow that was being inappropriate or whether it really was him, which is how I felt. I'll start paying attention to other casual street interactions, to see if they have any insight to offer me.

I discussed the event with my family. They told me not to worry about it and in the future, if a member of my family was nearby, I would not have any more problems. I'm not sure that's good enough though—if I'm doing something that means they have to watch over me, then maybe I'm doing something I shouldn't.

Aligning With Vision

Where are the gaps between my current reality and my vision of myself at my highest and best?

In a situation like this, where physical danger is a possibility, it can be difficult to align with my vision, which includes treating everyone with love and respect.

How does this situation confirm my vision? What aspects of my vision does it confirm?

I guess treating everyone with love and respect includes treating myself that way too. So putting greater distance between us would have been okay. And finding a new place to jump rope in the future would be part of that too— treating myself and maybe also treating local customs with love and respect.

How, if at all, does this critical moment experience suggest I change or refine my vision?

I need to be aware that respect may look different here than it does in the world I'm used to. I don't think the words of my vision need to change at all; I just need to broaden my understanding of what the words may really mean in practice.

And then... Discerning Right Action

What might I do to bring my current reality into alignment with my vision?

I can look for somewhere else to exercise, some place less visible to casual passersby.

What action might best move me towards my highest hopes and enhance the creative potential of this interaction, relationship, or situation?

I think I perhaps should have stopped jumping and said something very simple like "Como estas?" In doing so, I might have un-objectified myself and made the situation more personal, therefore harder for him to be so rude to me. I would have also removed the foreign act of jumping rope. Perhaps he would have been happy with me acknowledging him and he would have moved on with his friend.

What, if anything, is the right thing to do? To say? To whom? How?

It's hard for me to say in this situation what would have been the right thing to do. It's very clear that doing what I was doing—continuing to jump rope and ignore him—wasn't very effective. I think next time I might respond briefly and go back inside, and look for somewhere else to exercise in the future.

To Summarize

What have I learned about myself? What have I learned about the situation or other people involved?

What have I learned about what it means to be effective in situations of difference?

What have I learned about what it means to align with my highest and best?

What is my current energy state? Am I feeling inspired and energized?

Well I don't really like it, but I can tell it's right that I have to change what I'm doing: I can't keep jumping rope in public. I'll either have to find some other form of exercise while I'm here or find a private place to do it.

There's sort of a sense of internal relaxation that I have about it, like an "aha, well that's so obvious" kind of feeling.

THE POST OFFICE

by Megumi

Briefly summarize your Something's Up critical moment.

What are the circumstances? What happened?
Describe the situation with as little interpretation or evaluation as you possibly can.

I was facilitating a program for USAmericans on doing business in Japan, using an example from my own experience to illustrate the deeply rooted nature of gender hierarchy and the cultural idea still common in Japan that the head of the family must be male.

The core of the story is that the post office regularly added my male housemate's name to my mail, readdressing it in care of his name before delivering it to me, even though the apartment was registered with the post office under my name.

To me this very profound illustration showed the subtle ways in which something like gender hierarchy can manifest itself in cultural forms. But the program participants (mostly male) were uninterested in the story, even resistant to it.

I worked this CMD in the back of my mind, in the midst of my interaction with the participants in the training room. I wrote it down later and fleshed it out a bit, but the core PL Shift happened in the moment on the training floor.

Attending to Emotion

What are the positive or negative emotions I am having in this situation? What are the qualities and characteristics of my emotions?

Retelling the story to the room of participants, the situation again became deeply personal. I found myself getting angry again, again feeling self-righteous. I am tired of being discriminated against, even in subtle ways, just because I am a woman.

And then when the participants resisted the core insight being demonstrated by my story, I got even more angry and self-righteous! I also felt blocked, suddenly unsure in my role as a facilitator about how to reconnect them to the content.

What information are the emotions offering me?

The experience, even though it took place several years ago, is still quite alive in me!

I need to get my clarity around this story, release my own emotion, if I want to be able to use it with participants. I have to be able to talk with people about it even when they see the situation differently than I do.

Why do I care about this critical moment situation so much? Which of my values are involved?

I'm committed to gender equality, have a strong sense of social justice. If something is wrong, I want to fix it.

And as a Japanese woman working with these USAmerican participants, I also felt it my duty to show the real picture (not always rosy) of Japanese culture.

Attending to Judgment

What is the positive or negative judgment I am having about myself, or about the other person or situation I am facing?

The post office readdressed my mail in care of my male housemate based on the Japanese cultural assumption that the head of the family must be male.

Japanese cultural tradition still discriminates against women.

I am "just"; this discrimination is wrong.

What positive or negative assumptions am I making about myself, the other person, or the situation I am facing?

The post office did not know I was the actual head of household.

The post office would not have put his name on my mail for any reason other than reasons of gender discrimination.

My participants are sexist themselves for not immediately understanding the point of my story.

What was I expecting? What is motivating me in this situation? What do I think is motivating the other people involved?

I expected the participants to see that gender discrimination in Japanese culture is deeply rooted and can sneak up on you; it may not be as obvious as it once was but it still influences behavior in very direct ways. I expected that the participants would understand and support my anger, because they came from a culture with less gender hierarchy.

Attending to Physical Sensation

What is the physical sensation I'm experiencing in this critical moment situation? Where is the sensation located in my body?

As soon as I realized my example wasn't making the point I expected it to make with the participants, I felt my adrenalin rising. My blood pressure seemed to increase, my pulse to speed up.

What is the sensation about? What is it communicating to me?

I'm being driven by the emotion of this past situation, and am too off balance to work effectively with the participants, to take their resistance to the story and work it with them so that the learning nevertheless comes through.

What do I need to do to feel physically at ease and balanced again?

I need to free myself from the emotion, for sure. I'd love to jump up and down, move, but I'm in the midst of a training room surrounded by participants! I'll walk casually around the front of the room, take some centering breaths.

Engaging Ambiguity

What do I not know?

I don't know whether the post office did indeed put my housemate's name on my letters simply because his was a male name. Were they really practicing gender discrimination?

What more can I not know?

Is there any other reason the post office could possibly have put his name on my mail...?

As soon as I asked myself this question, I remembered that when I have presentations with my male co-facilitator, his name tends to be listed first—but in these instances it's because his last name starts with an "A" and mine starts with an "S" and we are listed in alphabetical order. And, so ... aha, my former housemate's last name also started with an "A." Suddenly I felt like laughing … the PL Shift was happening in me.

What can I do to become more comfortable with the ambiguity and/or to get some clarification?

If I really wish, I could ask the post office how they decide who is in care of whom when more than two family names are represented in a single apartment or house.

I still think my interpretation is the correct one, but now that I see the humor in the alphabetizing of the names, I acknowledge the probable gender discrimination without feeling the same kind of anger.

Cultivating Stillness

What additional questions, focusing on any of the practices, do I need to ask myself?

What do I want to do with my experience of the PL Shift around this experience? How does this fit with my vision?

Taking a breath, what insight comes from the silence within?

I got this one already! I took a breath to re-establish my physical balance, asked what else I could not know, and suddenly this other possibility came shooting into my awareness.

What can I learn about myself from this critical moment situation?

Emotion does sweep me away when the issue is so close to "home"!

Aligning With Vision

Where are the gaps between my current reality and my vision of myself at my highest and best?

Before the PL Shift, I was so entangled that I could not present the case very effectively to the participants. Every response I gave to their resistance simply created more resistance.

How does this situation confirm my vision? What aspects of my vision does it confirm?

In my vision, I write about "co-creating our own reality." This really reminds me that I can release my emotional response to gender discrimination and use my passion for gender equity and social justice more effectively.

How, if at all, does this critical moment experience suggest I change or refine my vision?

It doesn't!

And then... Discerning Right Action

What might I do to bring my current reality into alignment with my vision?

Relax into the example and the participants' resistance to it. Instead of resisting the resistance, work with it and "massage" around it until the core learning point is achieved.

What action might best move me towards my highest hopes and enhance the creative potential of this interaction, relationship, or situation?

Even if this post office practice is indeed an example of gender discrimination, I can deal with it not from the place of anger but from the place of humor. If I choose to tell the post office not to put me c/o a guy, I can be more effective: I will not accuse the post office, I will not make an enemy.

Perhaps I can help the post office realize their own gender-biased assumption. I will certainly be more effectively positioned to change gender discrimination practices.

What, if anything, is the right thing to do? To say? To whom? How?

To the post office, at this point, probably nothing. This has been more about my own learning, and especially about how I need to be more emotionally level about my experiences before I bring them into a training program to illustrate Japanese culture.

But we'll see—if some day my mail is again addressed to me care of a man, maybe I'll go talk with the post office about it!

To Summarize

What have I learned about myself? What have I learned about the situation or other people involved?

What have I learned about what it means to be effective in situations of difference?

What have I learned about what it means to align with my highest and best?

What is my current energy state? Am I feeling inspired and energized?

It's amazing how humor can sometimes allow us to keep a dual reality, holding both what we believe to be true and at the same time giving the possibility of an alternative explanation. It's interesting to consider how that might help us as we work to change some of the cultural aspects of our societies that we find personally offensive.

Co-Creating Meaning

by Adair

Briefly summarize your Something's Up critical moment.

What are the circumstances? What happened?
Describe the situation with as little interpretation or evaluation as you possibly can.

I have been preoccupied in the past weeks, and almost paralyzed by fear, about a personal situation that is extremely important to me but that I felt I could not influence. Every time I attempted to gain new clarity by doing a CMD on it, I got stuck. Each time, I found myself struggling with how to co-create meaning with the other people involved. There was a gap that I couldn't seem to overcome.

I decided to focus my attention on a different situation, a professional one rather than a personal one, where I am in fact very successful in co-creating meaning. I decided to do a CMD on the inspiring dimensions of that work. Perhaps it would help me understand what my two colleagues on that project, Kiyoko and Junko, and I actually do that allows us to co-create meaning. Perhaps I would be able to translate any insights I get from my professional environment into this other, personal, situation where I so need to have it. It would be interesting to see if it helped me bridge the gap. I asked another Personal Leadership practitioner, Elizabeth, to coach me through the CMD.

In this professional situation, I am part of a team implementing a three-year research project funded by a Japanese government grant (*kakenhi*). The purpose of the project is to formulate communication skill workshops for supporters of people who have experienced domestic violence. Kiyoko and Junko are very inspiring to me and we work well together.

Attending to Judgment

What is the positive or negative judgment I am having about myself, or about the other person or situation I am facing?

I am making an important, but different contribution to our project.
My co-researchers are doing the same, each in her own way.

What positive or negative assumptions am I making about myself, the other person, or the situation I am facing?

We are all capable and have valuable contributions to make.

We each respect what the other brings to the project.

What was I expecting? What is motivating me in this situation? What do I think is motivating the other people involved?

I expected to enjoy working on this socially important project with people I respect and like.

Attending to Emotion

What are the positive or negative emotions I am having in this situation? What are the qualities and characteristics of my emotions?

Excitement. Pride: we received the grant; we can make this potentially valuable contribution.

Gratitude to my Japanese colleagues for handling all the Japanese aspects of the project.

It's satisfying to connect with program interviewees.

What information are the emotions offering me?

Reinforcement to continue when my time may be more restricted in the coming two years of the grant.

Research provides me with the chance to interact with people I enjoy.

Why do I care about this critical moment situation so much? Which of my values are involved?

Service: making a difference! Appreciating the contribution of others.

Attending to Physical Sensation

What is the physical sensation I'm experiencing in this critical moment situation? Where is the sensation located in my body?

I am comfortable in our meetings. Even if I am overscheduled, I enjoy them and am energized and motivated to continue working on the project.

Combination of mentally stimulated, whole-body comfort, relaxation.

What is the sensation about? What is it communicating to me?

Continuing to invest my time and energy in this is worthwhile to me in addition to achieving the result.

What do I need to do to feel physically at ease and balanced again?

Remember to recognize and fully experience these sensations.

Cultivating Stillness

What additional questions, focusing on any of the practices, do I need to ask myself?

What am I learning about designing workshops that take people to a deep level?

What is it in our own experiences that allows us to feel closer to the people whom we are trying to assist?

What new possibilities emerge from this work?

Taking a breath, what insight comes from the silence within?

No matter how academic a project, the use of spiritual practice is relevant.

We can get caught in a negative loop and recycle violence or verbal abuse, re-traumatize ourselves by replaying it internally. I need to break the loop.

What can I learn about myself from this critical moment situation?

How to support myself when I'm in a situation that has a component of abuse, or how to seek an ally.

Engaging Ambiguity

What do I not know?

I don't know whether the limitations I feel will prove to be real. Can I lead a workshop in Japanese?

I don't know how much time I will have for this in the future.

Will we come up with something truly valuable?

What more can I not know?

None of us knows how much time we will have in the future.

What can I do to become more comfortable with the ambiguity and/or to get some clarification?

Keep communicating about time constraints we are each feeling.

Consciously develop the language I need to prepare and present specific exercises in this workshop.

Aligning With Vision

Where are the gaps between my current reality and my vision of myself at my highest and best?

Before I started, I knew I needed to learn more about co-creating meaning. This CMD has really helped me do that. Now I'm going to apply this to the challenging personal situation with which I've been struggling, and see how the learning can help me there.

How does this situation confirm my vision? What aspects of my vision does it confirm?

Co-creation is central to being able to work in a larger sphere.

How, if at all, does this critical moment experience suggest I change or refine my vision?

It doesn't seem necessary to do so.

And then... Discerning Right Action

What might I do to bring my current reality into alignment with my vision?

Consciously attend to the process of our research team collaboration. And consciously attend to the way I collaborate with the people involved in my personal situation too.

What action might best move me towards my highest hopes and enhance the creative potential of this interaction, relationship, or situation?

Redefine the priority this project has in my time allotment. What if I actually consider the other people involved in my personal situation as my allies rather than my obstacles, as people who also want to co-create meaning with me...?!

What, if anything, is the right thing to do? To say? To whom? How?

Be as flexible as I can.

Meet as often as possible and move this project forward to the greatest extent possible for all of us.

Share this CMD with Kiyoko and Junko and be open to their suggestions and perceptions.

And in terms of my personal situation, I'm ready to try a CMD on that situation again, now with this new insight. And the energy I feel about co-creating meaning is so strong, I'll hold that with me and let it guide me as I do that exploration.

To Summarize

What have I learned about myself? What have I learned about the situation or other people involved?

What have I learned about what it means to be effective in situations of difference?

What have I learned about what it means to align with my highest and best?

What is my current energy state? Am I feeling inspired and energized?

The energy that emerged from doing this CMD reflected what mattered most to me about this project. The energy felt solid and got me to the heart of what was important—(1) joy in working with my colleagues, and (2) focus on key approaches in the project itself, use of self-awareness and a combination of spiritual techniques.

Afterword

I used this CMD document with my two colleagues, Kiyoko and Junko, to review the first year of our research and articulate the vision of how we would move forward into our second and third years. We were all energized by sharing this way.

I asked Kiyoko and Junko if they would be willing to comment briefly on how the CMD worked for us as a review of our past year's work and as a way of strengthening our joint vision of the next one.

Kiyoko's comment: "When I first heard the term 'CMD', I found myself automatically associating it with a focus on something negative. Then when Adair shared this CMD with us, I was surprised and even excited to see how much this would fit in our project. Now, our schedule is becoming tighter and tighter, but somehow I have a feeling that we can work alright as I know we can work both independently and interactively."

Junko's comment: "When I was reading your CMD, I felt I would like to do mine. And I did, along with your CMD, which helped me a lot and made clear what I can do next."

These comments suggest the effect of this type of inspiring CMD and its natural movement outward in ever-widening circles as we all work at our edge.

The inspiring presence of these three extraordinary women—Elizabeth who coached me in the CMD and Kiyoko and Junko who work on the project with me—is an important component of the special energy the CMD regenerated in me; it has an uplifting effect whenever I just bring it to mind. For me, this is the nature of spiritual inspiration: it provides a mysterious energy when we most need it.

It also has a positively contagious quality: it has helped me to move into inspiration in the other, almost paralyzing, personal situation where I most felt the need for it.

PLAYING JAZZ

by Nathan

Briefly summarize your Something's Up critical moment.

What are the circumstances? What happened?
Describe the situation with as little interpretation or evaluation as you possibly can.

I recently watched a movie produced in the United States in 1959 called *The Cry of Jazz*. It presents a systematic analysis of the social forces that produced and continue to shape the genre of music we call jazz. The lead character, Alex, asserts that all the "basic and fundamental contributions to jazz have been made by Negroes" and that jazz is the musical expression of the Negro spirit being able to accept all the hazards of being Negro and simultaneously triumph over these hazards.

As a white musician with a substantial background in jazz, I know that jazz came out of the black experience, and my activism working on issues of racism has left me few illusions as to the suffering of blacks in the United States where jazz was born. I have heard the greats in jazz and know something of their lives; I see the connection with creativity often associated with the suffering of people on the margins of privilege. I have listened to music from white artists that seem to lack terribly in depth and soul; I see the disconnection with creativity often associated with the comforts of being in the mainstream. Yet in large part, I come from this privileged mainstream, from the sociopolitical status quo.

What this movie brought up for me is the question of my own depth as an artist, given my white, privileged, and status quo socialization. The question at times haunts me, and the movie brought it right to the forefront: is it really possible for me, as a white man schooled in jazz as academia (in other words, not in jazz as a creative response to suffering), to play this music rooted in blackness with honor, respect and dignity?

Attending to Physical Sensation

What is the physical sensation I'm experiencing in this critical moment situation? Where is the sensation located in my body?

I feel it in my head; it hurts.

What is the sensation about? What is it communicating to me?

If all I do is reproduce jazz from an academic position, I will not be respecting the spirit of jazz; however, if I create the music I play out of my own life experiences, tensions and resolutions, I will be playing reverently to my influence from jazz.

What do I need to do to feel physically at ease and balanced again?

Bring my attention to the rest of my body, and help my head reconnect.

Attending to Emotion

What are the positive or negative emotions I am having in this situation? What are the qualities and characteristics of my emotions?

The emotions that come up for me are fear and insecurity.

What information are the emotions offering me?

I have insecurity because I need to feel supported as an artist so that I can take the risks involved to find my voice and express it. Thinking that being of the dominant culture takes me away from even the possibility of expressing in this way removes that support.

I have fear because I have a need to live, work and play from this place of soul expression—and this kind of thinking says, "You'll never be able to!" It also says, "Even if you were able to, the people you care about wouldn't understand or care; or maybe they would, but only when you have perfected a brilliant *everything* musically."

Why do I care about this critical moment situation so much? Which of my values are involved?

Music is at the core of who I am, and so is acting with responsibility and integrity as a white man in a white-dominant racist world. This critical moment brings these two core values together into what feels like conflict.

Attending to Judgment

What is the positive or negative judgment I am having about myself, or about the other person or situation I am facing?

The judgment is, "You can't play like that, you're middle-class white." A variation is, "If you want to play like that, you're going to have to suffer."

What positive or negative assumptions am I making about myself, the other person, or the situation I am facing?

The assumptions I am making about myself through these judgments is that as a dominant-culture person, I cannot connect with soul and give it expression musically because I have been too coddled by status quo living.

The assumption about myself is that I have not and cannot expand myself beyond those limiting factors of my socialization, and that the factors are in fact limiting. The other assumption about myself is that I have not been, and am not, supported in my artist's journey. Finally, there is the assumption that I have to suffer in order to make "good art."

I'm also assuming that other people wouldn't understand or care about my music when I express from my soul; or maybe they would, once I reach my end product—blazing brilliance that no one could deny!

What was I expecting? What is motivating me in this situation? What do I think is motivating the other people involved?

I am expecting a certain kind of support, based on a quite inflexible definition of support.

Cultivating Stillness

What additional questions, focusing on any of the practices, do I need to ask myself?

Is this all true? Does this *feel* right? What is it about the black situation in the United States that brought forth this music, and what might that kind of connection with music be like from the current perspective of whites? What music is happening now by whites that contradicts the message that it's not possible to express for whites what jazz expressed for blacks, given our own set of circumstances?

Though I was raised in the status quo, what does my particular, unique experience, along with that of my fellow whites, offer me that I can connect with and express soulfully?

Taking a breath, what insight comes from the silence within?

I am doing it ... I am in the journey and I will find greater and greater connection with my unique voice musically.

The space this comes from is different than "jazz." The category is not of primary importance—the connection with community *and* individual voice is what is important.

What can I learn about myself from this critical moment situation?

I can learn to honor the expression of this internal critic, to befriend it, and to see it for what it is: an expression of personality. I can then connect with higher self and my vision and move to my next step.

Engaging Ambiguity

What do I not know?

I don't know that it can't be done. I don't know how people will respond to my musical expression, how it will or will not speak to them and move them.

What more can I not know?

I can "not know" what my particular journey will look like.

What can I do to become more comfortable with the ambiguity and/or to get some clarification?

I can recognize the journey involved in unfolding as an artist and honor that journey by letting go of the need to know and of the judgments as they come so that I can quickly realign with my next steps. I can also nurture my artist self and celebrate successes along the way!

Aligning With Vision

Where are the gaps between my current reality and my vision of myself at my highest and best?

The need to know—both the need to know what the future will look like, if I will "succeed," and the need to think I know what others are thinking or will think.

How does this situation confirm my vision? What aspects of my vision does it confirm?

In my vision of myself at my highest and best, I say that I bring my creativity to all that I do. In this situation, my vision guides me to embrace the process.

How, if at all, does this critical moment experience suggest I change or refine my vision?

This experience suggests I refine my vision to incorporate the following: "Primary to my spiritual, familial, and professional lives is the cultivation of my creativity. Through cultivating my own creativity, I help others engage their creativity. As we live more creatively, we help heal ourselves, others, and our world."

And then... Discerning Right Action

What might I do to bring my current reality into alignment with my vision? What action might best move me towards my highest hopes and enhance the creative potential of this interaction, relationship, or situation?
What, if anything, is the right thing to do? To say? To whom? How?

My right action is to refine my vision statement as noted above and to continue cultivating my creativity!

To Summarize

What have I learned about myself? What have I learned about the situation or other people involved?
What have I learned about what it means to be effective in situations of difference?
What have I learned about what it means to align with my highest and best?
What is my current energy state? Am I feeling inspired and energized?

I have learned—which is to say I have remembered with greater depth—that although we all have unique experiences and expressions of creativity, ultimately no one person or group has more access to creativity than another.

ABOUT THE AUTHORS

Drs. Barbara Schaetti, Sheila Ramsey, and Gordon Watanabe have been close colleagues and friends for more than 15 years. They first started working with the ideas of Personal Leadership in 1995, formally introduced the methodology of two principles and six practices in 1998, and have been actively involved in its ongoing evolution ever since.

Barbara F. Schaetti, Ph.D., is founder and principal of Transition Dynamics and a member of the faculty of the Intercultural Communication Institute. She is recognized worldwide for her work with expatriate family services, and for her commitment to helping people access their core intercultural capacity. Her professional philosophy is rooted in the transformative potential inherent in a life lived in the midst of difference and change. Barbara specializes in multicultural team development, expatriate and leadership coaching, and the development of a personal practice to leverage intercultural competence. She is qualified to facilitate the Intercultural Development Inventory and the Psych-K change process. A dual national (USAmerican and Swiss) raised in 10 countries on five continents, she is currently based in Seattle, Washington, USA. Barbara is one of the three originators of the Personal Leadership methodology, and serves as the Managing Director of Personal Leadership Seminars LLC.

Sheila Ramsey, Ph.D., is founder of The Crestone Institute, a Washington, DC-based consulting firm specializing in the interface between leadership and creativity. She is known internationally for her work in the field of intercultural relations and the facilitation of individual and group creativity. Since 1975, she has worked with leaders in the corporate sector, in government and in international development. In this work, she has seen how those who make a commitment to bring forth the highest and best in themselves are also those who are most creative in their own lives and most inspiring to others. She has been a professional photographer, studied as a potter's apprentice in Japan, is a visual artist, and is professionally certified in the Enneagram of Personality and is qualified in Psych-K. Sheila is one of the three originators of the Personal Leadership methodology.

 **Gordon Watanabe**, Ed.D., is Professor Emeritus and former Special Assistant to the President for Intercultural Relations at Whitworth University in Spokane, Washington, USA. He is a member of the faculty of the Intercultural Communication Institute and consults with corporate, community, and educational institutions. His work focuses on the critical role of deep self-understanding in successful cross-cultural negotiations and intercultural team building. Informed by his background as a third generation Japanese-American, and his years counseling international and U.S. ethnic minority students, Gordon is often called upon to be a cultural bridge between individuals and groups. He is a qualified Intercultural Development Inventory facilitator, Psych-K professional, and Energy-Meditation teacher. Gordon is one of the three originators of the Personal Leadership methodology.

What People Say About Personal Leadership
– the Methodology and the Book

Personal Leadership is a profound framework for continuously connecting to and aligning with one's personal wisdom, values, and vision on a day-to-day basis. In the midst of complexity, conflict, and change, Personal Leadership is easy to use and the most effective tool I've seen to help people access their authenticity. It's an anchor for anyone involved in making a difference and leading change in the world.

Elizabeth Robinson
Director, LeadChange
Washington, DC, USA

As an expatriate on the move, change has always been daunting and other cultures overwhelming, and no introductory course on a country can possibly prepare you for the physical and emotional stress change produces. Personal Leadership, however, has given me both the skills and the mindset to embrace the challenge change brings, allowing me to work with my fears and thus to transform them into curiosity, a chance to learn, and, most importantly, a chance to grow and develop as a citizen of the world. Using Personal Leadership, I have taken on new challenges, embraced new ways of thinking, and now can go out into the world, not without fear or uncertainty, but knowing that I have the ability to cope with whatever I meet.

Valerie Scane
Chair, School Council, Jakarta International School
Jakarta, Indonesia

Personal Leadership has given me a way to create a "home within." Whether I am packed into an overcrowded train in Tokyo or designing the most exciting training program with my colleagues, my vision and my practice of Personal Leadership keep me aligned with my deepest sources of inspiration. Reading this book not only introduces you to the methodology of Personal Leadership and how you can apply it; it also gives you a feel for what it's like to have your practice of Personal Leadership serve you as a guiding light.

Megumi Sugihara
Director, Personal Leadership Seminars—Japan
Tokyo, Japan

Personal leadership combines the dynamism of a whole systems design with the interiority of emotional intelligence. The result: emergent practical solutions in my work as an organization development consultant, and in my everyday life. A powerful approach!

Heather Robinson, MA
Founder and Principal Consultant, Success Across Borders
Seattle, Washington, USA

Personal Leadership offers us ways to work creatively in the moment with our lived experience, even when we feel at the edge of what we know and think we are capable of. The practice moves us from being stuck in resistance, into the liminal space of flow and learning that comes from inspiration. Personal Leadership, for me, is an integrative and transformative frame for my work with bodymindfulness, and can be applied in virtually any context.

Adair Linn Nagata, Ph.D.
Professor, Rikkyo Graduate School of Intercultural Communication
Trustee, The International House of Japan
Tokyo, Japan

Personal Leadership provides a deeply empowering experience. The astounding integrity and simplicity of this practice compels me to connect with my self— and to look not without, but within, where the truth lies. The purpose of this practice—to discover what is right, to exercise options—elevates it beyond any professional context. Personal Leadership is clearly my hope for making my world a better place to live.

Sreemathi Ramnath
Founder, "immer besser" Cross-Cultural Management Training Consultancy
President, Society for Intercultural Education, Training, and Research, India
Chennai, India

The Personal Leadership course we offer in our Master of Arts in Intercultural Relations program provides our students with an elegant way to translate the theory of the field into actual practice. The concepts and tools help them take responsibility for their own cultural values, bring them insight into their interactions with people from other cultures, and lead them to more competent ways of behaving in intercultural settings. Personal Leadership is a critical element in the success of our graduate program.

Kent Warren, Ph.D.
Director of Graduate Programs, Intercultural Communication Institute
Portland, Oregon, USA

The principles and practices of Personal Leadership have been taught and practiced in the Master in Teaching program at Whitworth University since 1997. Utilizing Personal Leadership's Critical Moment Dialogue (CMD), our teacher candidates reflect upon and write about a real-life teaching-specific critical moment. This provides documented evidence that our candidates are beginning to take responsibility for their own biases and dispositions across difference, and how both can influence the decisions they make as members of a multicultural learning community.

David Cherry, Ph.D.
Director, Master in Teaching program, School of Education, Whitworth University
Spokane, Washington, USA

"Umtu ungumtu ngabantu: a person is a person through other persons" (Xhosa saying). Personal Leadership shows people how to apply theories about teams and intercultural communication to their personal and professional situations. It helps leaders and members of multicultural teams acknowledge their own contributions, and trust others whose skills and strengths are different. In this way, a multicultural team becomes an incredible source of richness and energy.

Véronique Schoeffel
Training Coordinator, CINFO
Bienne, Switzerland
(Centre d'information, de conseil et de formation. Professions de la coopération internationale.
Center for Information, Counseling and Training. Professions in International Cooperation.)

Personal Leadership has proven to be a powerful tool in student leadership training with our U.S. multicultural students, our dominant-culture students, and our international student leaders. It also serves students in our semester-long study abroad trip to Central America, where studies and activities expose them to a range of cultural, language, political, social, religious, and economic environments. Personal Leadership presents all these students with a process for developing and aligning with their personal vision statement and a methodology to self-adjust, self-correct, and adapt to the multitude of situations they encounter. The PL curriculum has helped our students transform their lives.

Esther Louie
Assistant Dean, Intercultural Student Affairs, Whitworth College
Spokane, Washington, USA

Working with the Personal Leadership methodology has significantly enhanced my professional life, inside and outside of the training room, and inspires me to be more fully present and resourceful when teaching, training, and coaching across cultures. Practicing Personal Leadership has become much more than an area of interest for me; it has become a way to live in a multicultural world and a means by which to approach challenges and to build lasting and fulfilling relationships. The authors of this inspiring book embody the Personal Leadership practice as a way of life and their example will surely inspire all who read it.

Jan O'Brien
Principal Consultant, Jan O'Brien & Associates
Houston, Texas, USA

Personal Leadership is a powerful vehicle that enables positive relationships within groups, organizations or communities. As a management consultant for organizational change, I have found the practices of benefit to my clients. They have also had a positive impact on the way in which I interact with people both personally and professionally. This simple, usable system can benefit anyone.

Joanne Daykin
Principal, Innovation Partners International
Ottawa, Ontario, Canada

I practice Personal Leadership to maximize my effectiveness as a global business consultant, to help my clients reach their goals in the multinational workplace. This well-written and engaging book explains the principles and practices of Personal Leadership, step by step, inviting the reader to live a more aware life. An abundance of rich and colorful stories in each chapter illustrate the "workings" of Personal Leadership and make the methodology come to life. Personal Leadership is a handy resource for those who want to "wake up" and make a difference—day by day!

Rita Wuebbeler
Founder and President, Interglobe Cross-Cultural Business Services, Inc.
Atlanta, Georgia, USA

How to Find a Personal Leadership Seminar
and Join the Community of Practice

If you are new to the methodology of Personal Leadership, and if what you have read here has drawn you to develop a personal practice, we encourage you to participate in a seminar. The activities, discussions, and community that the seminars offer will magnify your understanding and integration of the methodology.

Personal Leadership seminars are offered in three primary ways:

1. As public events sponsored by Personal Leadership Seminars LLC. At the time of publication, these events are held annually in Crestone, Colorado, USA; annually in Kyoto, Japan; and periodically in Europe.

2. As public events sponsored by other organizations, such as the Summer Institute for Intercultural Communication (SIIC).

3. As private events contracted for by clients, and typically addressing a particular focus such as team building, leadership development, the building of inclusive community, expatriate family preparation, study abroad programming, and international student services.

Personal Leadership is also offered through one-on-one personal and/or professional coaching.

You can access a list of recognized Personal Leadership facilitators on our website. These facilitators are the only people authorized to facilitate Personal Leadership programs, and indeed are the only ones with the training and preparation to do so.

If you are reading this book in conjunction with a Personal Leadership Foundations seminar or its equivalent, please join the worldwide community of Personal Leadership practitioners. Visit our website to find out how.

Information on becoming a recognized facilitator of Personal Leadership programs, as well as about our Training of Facilitators protocol and developmental benchmarks, is also available online.

www.plseminars.com

CPSIA information can be obtained at www.ICGtesting.com
Printed in the USA
LVOW10s0322180516

488730LV00006B/6/P